"*Transformed by Grace* brings you on the difficult journey away from a life of addiction, through the powerful grace of God. Laced with Scriptures and vivid analogies, it shows you the redemption you can have through Christ, without ignoring the hard truths that come alongside this transformation. Filled with thought-provoking reflection questions and action steps to fully engage the reader, perfect for individuals and recovery groups alike!"

—**MONICA ANDERSEN**, Healthcare Quality
and Clinical Excellence Leader

"The journey to sobriety involves many tools and steps along the way. It is a journey worth taking, but you'll need help to get there. In this book, Rodney shares wisdom from his experiences and uses helpful lessons from Scripture to guide you toward a life that is free from addiction. The reward is beyond measure. Let this book help guide and equip you in a way that you have prayed for. God is with you!"

—**NICK DEFORD**, Pastor, Zephyrhills First
Church of the Nazarene, Florida

"As a priest and pastor, I am quite familiar with the way people usually speak and write about grace, and I am happy that this book offers something beyond that. Here you will find a discovery of life and strength that defined themselves as grace for Rodney by liberating him from addiction. Even more impressively, Rodney shows in these pages how essential community is for recovery by telling his story always as a part of everyone's story—a story that has been unfolding for as long as people have cried out to God for deliverance. I heartily recommend this sincere and honest account to all who feel weak or hopeless."

—**ALLAN TUPA**, Pastor, St. Joseph Catholic
Church, Zephyrhills Florida

"This book is a rare gift—honest, scripturally grounded, and full of grace. It speaks to the heart of transformation: faith is more than belief—it's a radical commitment to action. As a scholar and a person of faith, I believe anyone navigating recovery will find wisdom, hope, and purpose in these pages."

—**CHRISTA REMINGTON**, Director, Center
for Leadership Research and Action

"*Transformed by Grace* is a highly readable spiritual account of one man's journey as he moved from addiction to individual freedom and the word of God to find strength, positivity, and redemption. Rodney Corriveau takes us with him on his journey, supported by Scriptures and resilience, using Christ's teachings as he changed his habits and his life. With Psalm 84:10 as a guide, the book is a scriptural path to sobriety offering advice, metaphors, and reflective opportunities for the reader."

—**STEVEN F. SPINA**, Retired City Manager, Zephyrhills, Florida

"*Transformed by Grace* is a radiant testimony of what it means to walk boldly in faith, led by love and purpose. Rodney's words are not just stories—they are seeds of wisdom, sown through a life of obedience, transformation, and service. As someone who believes in the power of resilience (*ñeque*) and grace, I found his journey deeply moving and incredibly relevant for anyone answering a call higher than themselves. His vulnerability is refreshing, his strength is gentle, and his devotion to living the Gospel with integrity reminds me that leadership isn't about position—it's about surrender and impact. This is not just a book; it's a beacon for anyone who desires to lead with a servant's heart, grow through challenges, and be transformed by the unshakable joy of saying 'yes' to God. Read it. Reflect. And let it stir something holy and powerful within you."

—**ROSIE PAULSEN**, Business Strategist

"*Transformed by Grace*—what can I say? Simply exceptional. Each page is steeped in emotion, honesty, and transformation. The depth of feeling woven into the writing resonates powerfully. A truly moving and unforgettable read. It touched me right where I was—in the middle of my mess, in need of something deeper. It reached a part of my soul that needed healing, and I didn't even know how much I needed that until I felt it. Truly life-giving."

—**BETH AKER**, Director, Meals On Wheels

Transformed by Grace

Transformed by Grace

A Scriptural Path to Sobriety

Rodney V. Corriveau

Foreword by Francesca L. Stubbs

RESOURCE *Publications* · Eugene, Oregon

TRANSFORMED BY GRACE
A Scriptural Path to Sobriety

Resource Publications
An Imprint of Wipf and Stock Publishers
199 W. 8th Ave., Suite 3
Eugene, OR 97401

www.wipfandstock.com

PAPERBACK ISBN: 979-8-3852-4512-3
HARDCOVER ISBN: 979-8-3852-4513-0
EBOOK ISBN: 979-8-3852-4514-7

VERSION NUMBER 07/18/25

To my family:

Thank you for your endless prayers and unwavering support through every step of my journey—from active addiction to recovery.

To those struggling:

May you find strength, hope, and healing. You are not alone.

Contents

Foreword

EVERY BELIEVER REACHES A pivotal moment when they understand that grace is far more than a concept. It's not just a means of forgiveness or a spiritual fallback; it's the divine force that transforms us from within. *Transformed by Grace* is a crucial and timely reflection on this life-changing reality.

In a world where we often measure ourselves by performance, perfection, and striving, this book warmly invites us to refocus on what truly transforms us: the unearned, unstoppable grace of God. Through each chapter, you'll explore how grace works in our lives—not as an excuse for complacency, but as the catalyst for living righteously, courageously, and authentically.

The author blends deep theological insights with heartfelt personal experience. With clarity and compassion, *Transformed by Grace* shows how grace renews our minds, reshapes our identities, and realigns us with our divine purpose. It encourages us to shed the masks we wear and embrace the freedom that only grace can offer.

Whether you're new to faith and looking for a solid foundation, a long-time believer in need of refreshment, or a leader wanting to guide others from a place of grace, this resource is guaranteed to speak life, encouragement, and strength all while giving each reader the necessary steps to freedom and wholeness. It promises to meet you where you are and carry you further than you ever thought possible.

So, take a deep breath and dive in. Release the burden of striving and let the grace of God transform you from the inside out.

—Dr. Francesca L. Stubbs
Global Speaker, Leadership Trainer & Author
Senior Pastor, Oasis Church at Zephyrhills
Visionary Leader—OAPN Global Network

Acknowledgments

FIRST AND FOREMOST, I thank God—for the grace, strength, and renewal that sustained me throughout this journey.

I am eternally grateful to Father Allan Tupa, whose spiritual insight was invaluable, and to Pastor Nick Deford, whose guidance played a vital role in advancing this work. Their support has been immeasurable.

A sincere thank you to John Chaplick for his honest critiques, which provided both direction and motivation, and to Mark Malatesta, whose feedback gave me the courage to keep going.

Sister Nancy has been a constant source of encouragement throughout my writing journey.

I am also deeply appreciative of Wipf and Stock Publishers for recognizing my potential as a new author, and to my copy editor, Riley Bounds, whose meticulous work was essential in bringing everything together.

Lastly, a special thanks to my mom—for patiently reviewing countless drafts over the years. You've always believed in me. You're the best.

PRAYER OF THE LOWLY DRUG ADDICT

Dear LORD,

I don't even know if I believe in you these days—but please save
    me from myself.

Save my soul from the destruction of my choices.

Walk with me in despair until I'm ready for your light.

Your ways are perfect and true—help me to never lose sight.

As I partake in my daily ritual, I plead for your patience.

Do not let this be my last time, because I'm not ready to meet you.

I think I still hate you—but I know I hate myself.

What started out as such an adventure has now bound me in chains.

Please lead me out of this darkness, and into your healing grace.

Though I've wandered far, I still know all glory, honor, and praise
    belong to you.

Introduction

WHAT IF YOUR STORY of addiction could be rewritten—not just to free you from substance abuse but to embrace an entirely new life, fully immersed in God's grace? *Transformed by Grace* demonstrates that true healing goes far beyond breaking the chains of addiction. Sobriety is a crucial first step, but the ultimate goal is wholeness—through the renewal of your body, mind, and spirit.

Recovery is more than changing behaviors; it's a deeply spiritual journey that realigns your life with the abundance found in Christ. As you walk this path, you'll discover that God's grace is not only the answer to your struggles—it is the foundation for a new life, one where every part of your being is fully restored through his power.

This book is a guide to sobriety and a companion on your walk with the LORD. Each chapter unpacks powerful biblical truths that address the internal battles you face in overcoming addiction. Along with these teachings, you'll find practical tools for inspiration and strength. Whether you're grappling with shame, isolation, fear, or temptation, these Scriptures offer a life-changing message of hope, strength, and resilience. God's word becomes your steadfast anchor amid the stormy seas of addiction, reminding you that you are never alone and are deeply loved by your Creator.

Recovery involves challenges, but it holds the promise of transformation when you surrender your will to God. To support your journey, *Transformed by Grace* includes reflection questions designed to help you apply the principles explored in each chapter to your own life. These questions will assist you in releasing your personal intentions in favor of God's perfect plan.

At the conclusion of each chapter, the *Faith in Action* section offers practical steps, enabling you to put these principles into practice. By engaging with these action points, you align yourself with God's renewal and healing, growing closer to him and becoming the person he created you to be.

As you immerse yourself in these pages, you will be inspired to trust in God's divine timing. No matter how intense your trials may seem, God's power is far greater and will carry you through every hardship in his ideal time. You'll come to understand that true recovery leads to a life of prosperity and freedom in the LORD.

Your past does not define you—God's grace does. His boundless love will free you from addiction's grip, filling you with peace, joy, and an eternal purpose beyond anything you can imagine!

1

The Illusion of Freedom

IN THE BEGINNING, THE escape promised by drugs and alcohol may seem like a brief taste of freedom. The reasons we turn to substances are unique to each of us; but for many, it begins as a get-away—relief from the burdens of daily struggles, liberation from the realities of life, and a release from inner turmoil. Our poison of choice comes in various forms, such as a drink, pill, or hit. Each one gleams like a golden light, allowing our cares and concerns to drift away like an untethered boat floating down a gently flow-ing stream. During that time, the world softens, and we believe we've unlocked the secret to peace, contentment, and joy. It feels like we've found the ultimate remedy for our troubles—a magical retreat offering the serenity we've longed for.

But over time, the initial euphoria begins to fade. The golden glow dims, and what once felt like freedom slowly transforms into a relentless pursuit of something just out of reach. Peace, once taken for granted, becomes more elusive. We think it's just around the next bend. But the high that once allowed our worries to drift downstream now pushes us toward a rapidly approaching water-fall. We're left chasing that fleeting feeling over and over—just to feel normal or stave off the suffocating fog of withdrawal. The joy that once comforted us fades, replaced by a hollow craving that is never truly satisfied. Little by little, we come to a painful realization: we're no longer in control. The habit has become an addiction. The substances have taken control of us.

We begin to sacrifice everything we once held dear—relationships, dreams, and even our sense of self—just to feed the insatiable hunger within. Our bodies grow weary and exhausted from the unending cycle while our minds become clouded, making it harder to think clearly. Each day, we wake up burdened by regret and guilt, only to drown it out once more with the very thing that keeps us trapped.

In moments of clarity, we feel the sharp contrast between who we are now and who we once were—the person we were before addiction took hold. But those times are short-lived. The remorse and shame of losing control weigh heavily on our hearts, yet the addiction pulls us back deeper into the abyss, further away from the peace and freedom we long for and closer to the approaching waterfall.

THE CYCLE OF TORMENT

What once seemed like a harmless way to cope with life's challenges soon proves to be an illusion. Addiction becomes a twisted ritual—a relentless cycle of torment that consumes us from the inside out. As we chase an unattainable and temporary pleasure, we find ourselves trapped in a never-ending loop, sinking deeper into despair. In the grip of addiction, there is no rest—no peace, no contentment, and no true comfort.

This cycle reflects the lies of the dark angel—the master of deception. He entices mankind with endless promises of pleasure but conceals the eventual consequences. As users, we feel empowered and in control in the beginning; we believe we're living in the light—and life seems good. We convince ourselves that we can stop whenever we choose and that we are the ones calling the shots. But slowly, what seemed like a release becomes a suffocating chain, binding us to an inescapable reality. What we once believed was serenity becomes the force that slowly destroys us—it's a cruel deception. As Jesus warns us in Matt 6:22–23, "The eye is the lamp of the body. So, if your eye is sound, your whole body will be full of light; but if your eye is not sound, your whole body will be full of darkness. If then the light in you is darkness, how great is the darkness!" The deeper we sink into addiction and darkness, the clearer it becomes: what was once believed to be freedom is actually a prison. We look into the mirror and see eyes that at one time sparkled with life—but are now hollow and drained of hope.

The pursuit of temporary happiness through substances is a dangerous trade-off. With every dose, we give up more of ourselves, eventually surrendering even our souls. The more we indulge, the more we fall into darkness—a deep darkness we once mistook for light. Addiction is not merely a physical dependence; it is a spiritual surrender to the lies Satan whispers in our ear. He doesn't only want our actions or bodies—he wants our hearts, minds, and the very essence of who we are. When addiction takes root, we become trapped in a cycle that intensifies with each use.

THE FALSE PROMISE OF INSTANT GRATIFICATION

As we use substances—and eventually abuse them—we become ensnared in the relentless pursuit of instant gratification. Each temporary fix promises comfort and enjoyment but ultimately fails to provide lasting fulfillment. We fixate on chasing fleeting highs, believing they will fill the emptiness within us. But it is in our desperate search for immediate satisfaction that the enemy traps us in a counterfeit comfort—an imitation of the true peace and joy that only God can offer. The cycle of addiction conditions us to seek temporary relief, causing us to doubt the enduring peace that Christ alone provides.

Each time we chase the short-lived pleasure of drugs or alcohol, we reinforce the wall between ourselves and the true freedom found in the LORD. The high may provide momentary relief, but it is merely a distraction—a temporal mask for the pain we feel. The truth is, substances cannot heal our wounds; only God's love has the power to reach the depths of our souls and heal our afflictions.

THE HOPE OF CHRIST'S REDEMPTION

There is hope. No matter how deep the pit we find ourselves in has become, Christ is the cure for darkness. The promises offered by substances are deceptions crafted by the enemy. These temporary moments of relief cloud our judgment and ultimately lead us further away from the true source of eternal peace. As we come to recognize the cost of our choices, we realize that the light we once sought was, in fact, darkness—it offers no lasting fulfillment. We have been deceived. But the LORD is the antidote—Jesus is the ultimate source of peace, and his power is far greater than any hold darkness may have on us.

In Mark 5:9, we witness Christ's divine power at work as he heals a man tormented by a legion of demons. No matter how many forces of darkness conspire against us, they are powerless against Jesus. When we arm ourselves with Christ and align our lives with him as our Savior, he will break the chains of addiction and free us from the bondage of substances.

If he can heal a man possessed by multiple demons, he is more than capable of healing us from the disease of addiction—if we choose to let him. Even in our deepest despair and darkest moments, God understands us better than the enemy ever could. When we surrender to him, the LORD will remove negative influences from our lives and guide us into a relationship with him, one that offers far more than the empty promises of drugs and alcohol. In place of cravings and dysfunction, we will experience Christ's perfect love.

In the book of John, Jesus instructs us, "Do not labor for the food which perishes, but for the food which endures to eternal life, which the Son of man will give to you; for on him has God the Father set his seal" (John 6:27). Our addiction to substances is a pursuit of what perishes—we chase after things that can never truly satisfy, ultimately leading us to destruction. But Jesus calls us to seek life through him, fully aware of our vulnerability to the distractions of this world. Fruitless labors do not bring us closer to the LORD; instead, they lead us astray. We must stay vigilant against this illusion of happiness throughout our human experience. When we allow Christ to armor us, we're empowered to live fully protected by him.

THE POWER OF REDEMPTION AND TRANSFORMATION

Lasting change begins when we acknowledge the nature of our addiction and turn to Christ for help. The moment we step into his true light, our redemption begins. God's love for us is unconditional, no matter how far we've fallen or how deep our addiction has taken us. In Rom 5:20, Paul proclaims, "Law came in, to increase the trespass; but where sin increased, grace abounded all the more." The deeper we have fallen, the greater the depth of God's grace is for us. It's in our darkest moments that we can experience the most profound transformation—when we open ourselves to God's grace.

Those who have dwelled in darkness understand how precious the light is when we finally encounter and embrace it. Our past struggles, though agonizing, can become the catalyst for embracing a new life. We can become living testimonies of God's grace, shining as beacons of hope to those still trapped in the cycle of addiction and dependency. As we walk in the light of Christ, we can guide others toward the serenity we have found.

Jesus assures us in John 8:12, "I am the light of the world; he who follows me will not walk in darkness, but will have the light of life." In Christ, we are set free from darkness and empowered to walk in the light of his love—not by our own strength but by his grace.

Once we step into the LORD's light, we are forever changed. Our journey from the emptiness of addiction to the fullness of recovery is not just about overcoming darkness or breaking free from self-destructive behavior—it's about being transformed by the power of God's love. Christ liberates and sustains us as we move from active addiction and into the fullness of freedom he has promised.

But before we can fully embrace this freedom, we must confront the patterns that led us to the darkness in the first place. Addiction often traps us in a cycle of self-destruction—habits and choices that keep us bound, even when we desire release. Understanding this cycle is key to breaking free so that we can live in the true light.

REFLECTION QUESTIONS

1. Acknowledging the Darkness and Letting Christ into Your Heart: Have you fully acknowledged the areas of darkness in your life where you need God's healing? Are you willing to invite the light of Christ into every corner of your heart, including those you've kept hidden? How does it feel to accept the truth that God's love for you is unconditional, no matter your circumstances?

2. False Promises and Recognizing the Path to Darkness: What false promises of quick relief or instant gratification have you believed in the past? How have they led you deeper into the darkness of addiction? What would it look like to reject these false paths and trust in Christ's eternal, unwavering truth and peace instead?

3. Seeking Christ's Light and Trusting His Transforming Grace: What specific steps can you take each day to intentionally seek the light of Christ? How can you stay focused on his grace and truth when the temptation to return to old habits arises? What actions can you commit to in order to allow Christ's transforming power to break the hold of addiction in your life?

FAITH IN ACTION: THE ILLUSION OF FREEDOM

Imagine you're lost in a dense forest. The trees loom tall around you, and the daylight is quickly fading into dusk. The path you once thought you knew is now obscured by the thick underbrush, and the shadows seem to stretch endlessly, making you feel small, unsure, and trapped. Each step forward only seems to pull you deeper into confusion.

At first, you might convince yourself that you're fine—that you can figure this out on your own, that you don't need any help. The darkness around you is uncomfortable, but it's manageable. You think you can continue wandering, that you can control your direction, just as someone might feel they can control their addiction. There's a false sense of freedom in that belief, the illusion that you're in control. But as time passes, the forest feels more suffocating, the dusk turns to a bleak darkness, and the path forward becomes more uncertain. You realize that what you thought was freedom was merely an illusion, keeping you stuck and lost.

Then, in the distance, a faint light flickers—so subtle at first that you wonder if you're imagining it. But there's something about it that pulls you in. It's not blindingly bright, but it's a light nonetheless, offering hope and a sense of direction. In the midst of the overwhelming darkness, it beckons you toward the truth that has been there all along.

What do you do?

You have a choice: remain where you are, caught in the darkness that keeps you lost, or take a step toward that light. The first option feels safe—it's comfortable, and even though it's leading you deeper into the shadows, it's all you've known for a very long time. But the light calls you toward something greater, something real. It invites you to trust, to step forward in faith, even though you don't know the exact path ahead.

This is how faith works in your journey of recovery. Addiction often comes with many falsities, such as the illusion of freedom. We believe we have control over our choices, but the reality is that we're caught in a cycle of self-destruction, unable to break free on our own. The substances we turn to may feel like an escape, but they only trap us deeper. Real freedom, however, is found in surrendering to God and trusting in his guidance.

Just as you must choose to step toward the light in the forest, you must choose to trust in God's direction. It's a process of letting go of your plans and taking action in faith, even when it's hard to see the way forward. Each step you take toward God's light is an act of trust that leads you out of the darkness and toward healing. In his presence, there is true freedom—freedom from the chains of addiction and the illusion of self-sufficiency.

Faith is not just a belief but a step forward. Just like taking that first step toward the light, it requires trusting that God's path is better than the illusion of control you've been holding onto. The LORD offers you a way out of the darkness, a path that leads to freedom and wholeness. As you trust him with your next steps, you'll experience the transformation he has for you.

1. Recognize the Illusions in Your Life

Action Step: Acknowledge where you've been holding on to false freedoms or trying to control things on your own. Reflect on the comfort these patterns bring even though they keep you stuck in darkness. This may require you to be brutally honest with yourself. Identify the ways you may have been using substances, behaviors, or coping mechanisms to mask pain or escape reality. Ask God to reveal these illusions in your life and give you the strength to face them head-on.

Personal Reflection: When I was caught in the throes of opioid addiction, I believed I was making progress toward recovery by numbing myself further with anxiety medication and alcohol. I was trapped in a vicious cycle where each attempt to escape the pain only deepened my entrenchment in my issues. I was blind to the destructive patterns that I was reinforcing and tone-deaf to the cries of my loved ones who were desperately trying to help me. My life was so chaotic that I couldn't see that the "freedom" I thought I was gaining through substances was, in reality, just another form of imprisonment. It wasn't until I faced the raw truth of my illusions that I was able to take the first step toward real freedom.

Why It Matters: Understanding that what feels comfortable isn't always the path to freedom helps you recognize the need for change. So often, the things we hold on to—the substances, distractions, or unhealthy coping mechanisms—can seem to offer temporary relief. But in reality, they only deepen the darkness in our lives. By acknowledging these illusions and surrendering them to God, we open ourselves to true freedom. This freedom is not about control or comfort; it's about trusting God and surrendering our will to his plan, knowing that his ways are always higher and better than our own.

2. Step Toward the Light in Faith

Action Step: Take a small step forward, even if the path ahead is unclear. Trust the light you see in the distance and move toward it, believing that God is guiding you, even when you can't see the entire way. Start with one small action—whether it's making a healthier choice, reaching out for support, or even taking a moment to pray. No matter how uncertain or challenging the step seems, trust that God will meet you in it and provide the strength and direction you need.

Why It Matters: Moving toward God's light requires trust. It can be scary to step forward when you don't have a clear map of the road ahead. But trusting in God's light, even in the smallest of actions, allows you to move closer to the healing and restoration he promises. The light represents the promise of a new life in Christ, a life full of hope, growth, and freedom. Every step you take in faith, no matter how small, brings you closer to the life God is calling you to—a life filled with purpose, peace, and his transformative power.

3. Embrace Trust over Certainty

Action Step: Release the need for control and certainty over every detail of your life. Trust in God's timing and his plan for you, knowing that he will lead you to what is best, even when the path ahead feels unclear. Surrender the pressure to have all the answers right now. Instead, take one step at a time, relying on God's wisdom and his perfect plan. Trust that he is guiding you, even when you can't see the entire way forward.

Why It Matters: Trusting God over your own need for control opens the door to peace and transformation. When you trust in God's timing and plan, you no longer have to carry the weight of trying to figure it all out on your own. Instead, you can rest in the assurance that God is in control, even when you can't see the full picture. This trust is the foundation of your new life. As you embrace it, you begin to experience a peace that transcends your circumstances and trust that he is leading you to a future that is far better than anything you could have orchestrated on your own.

Faith is more than belief; it is a commitment to action. Like stepping toward the light, faith requires that you trust God's path for you, even when the way forward seems uncertain. As you move through the steps of recognizing the illusion of control, stepping into the light, and embracing trust over certainty, you are not just moving toward freedom—you are walking with God toward your true purpose. This journey isn't about having all the answers or controlling every detail. It's about surrendering to God, who knows the way, trusting that his plan for you is better than any path you've tried to navigate on your own.

As you put your faith into action, know that the LORD will guide each step, leading you out of darkness and into his abundant life. Trust him with your next steps.

2

The Cycle of Self-Destruction

IN THE WISDOM OF Sirach 10:29,[1] Ben Sira asks two profound questions: "Who will justify the man that sins against himself? And who will honor the man that dishonors his own life?"

These questions strike at the heart of addiction, reflecting the internal battle we face every day. Every time we use, we unknowingly participate in an act of self-destruction. The substances we turn to become both our refuge and our downfall. The temporary relief they provide feels like an escape—an illusion of peace that masks the weight of guilt, shame, and regret. But each high is a hollow victory—one that slowly drains our soul and pulls us deeper into an endless cycle of torment and despair.

THE ILLUSION OF CONTROL

The cycle of addiction is like a shattered mirror, reflecting the very essence of self-destruction. At first, it seems manageable, offering an escape from the pain or discomfort of life. But over time, the

1. Regarded as apocryphal in most Protestant traditions; considered deuterocanonical in Catholic and Orthodox traditions.

cracks deepen, and the reflection grows more distorted. What once appeared as a solution now reveals itself as a prison, trapping us in a relentless loop of false hope, guilt, and despair. We convince ourselves that we're in control—that we can stop whenever we want, that the mirror can be repaired. But the truth is, addiction quickly transforms into a cruel master.

The substances that at one time assured us freedom now only tighten the chains that bind us. They deliver emptiness and pull us deeper into a pit of self-loathing while we dishonor ourselves. The more we chase the high, the further we drift from the person we once were. Over time, the weight of addiction becomes unbearable, and life itself feels nearly intolerable.

The hallmark of this unrelenting, recurring cycle is hopelessness—the complete absence of hope. The pursuit of a high—whether through alcohol, drugs, or any other form of escape—becomes a ritual, a pattern we repeat over and over, believing that this time will be different. Yet, the high no longer satisfies as it once did; joy and freedom have faded. In our desperate attempts to escape the realities of life, we dishonor the very essence of who we are.

THE CALL TO SURRENDER: THE BEGINNING OF HEALING

Despite the overwhelming darkness, a quiet whisper of truth persists. Beneath the suffocating haze of addiction, there is a voice calling us to something greater—something beyond the short-lived highs. Even in our deepest despair, we are gently reminded that we were made for more than the empty existence we've settled for. This truth calls us to healing and restoration, urging us to look past the desires of the flesh and toward lasting fulfillment that can only be found in God.

Addiction, though it distorts our lives and relationships, does not have the final say. True transformation begins when we surrender ourselves to the LORD. The moment we release the illusion of control, we unlock the door to real, lasting healing. By letting go of the belief that we can manage our own lives, we create space for

God's grace to work in us, initiating liberation and restoration that we could never achieve on our own.

Addiction thrives in secrecy and self-reliance, deceiving us into thinking we must face it alone. It whispers that no one—perhaps not even God—can truly understand our struggles or offer help. Trapped in this lie, we imprison ourselves with shame and deceit, desperately clinging to the illusion of control. We wear a mask for the world, while inside, we're quietly unraveling. The substances we turn to act as a wrecking ball, slowly demolishing everything we've fought to protect. No matter how hard we try to hold it together, the facade inevitably crumbles. In the end, we fall victim to the destructive forces of addiction, powerless to escape the devastation it spreads throughout every part of our lives.

SELF-RESPECT AND THE POWER OF SURRENDER

When we surrender to God, we open the door for his healing truth and forgiveness to flood our hearts. It is through this act of yielding that we finally gain the strength to break free, empowered by God's limitless grace. As Isa 55:7 says, "Let the wicked forsake his way, and the unrighteous man his thoughts; let him return to the LORD, that he may have mercy on him, and to our God, for he will abundantly pardon." In turning to God, we not only receive his mercy but also his supreme power to restore us fully, shattering the chains of addiction.

Addiction distorts our sense of self-worth, causing us to question whether we are worthy of love, respect, or healing. We may wonder how others can honor us when we struggle to honor ourselves. However, the first step toward recovery is not about seeking approval from others or trying to prove our worth—it begins with opening ourselves to God's grace and allowing him to work within us. Everlasting healing is found in his mercy when we turn to the LORD, surrender our doubts, and allow his love to restore our sense of value and purpose.

Just as a weary swimmer caught in turbulent waters cannot save himself without help, we too cannot break free from the grip of addiction on our own. In our attempts to stay afloat, we often become exhausted and feel hopeless, convinced that there's no escape. Yet, the lifeline is always within reach—God's loving hand, extended to pull us from the depths of despair. When we feel as though we are drowning under the weight of addiction, we can reach out to him. God will lift us to safety, steady our hearts, and begin the healing process. Trusting in his path to freedom means taking his hand, knowing he will lead us to the liberty we long for.

Psalm 16:11 offers us wisdom and guidance in following the LORD: "You show me the path of life; in your presence there is fulness of joy, in your right hand are pleasures for evermore."

This verse reminds us that when we follow the LORD, he leads us on a path to true life filled with his promise of eternal pleasures. It's a gentle invitation to surrender our own efforts to find satisfaction and allow God to fill us with the true, lasting joy that only he can provide. As we trust in him, he guides us toward a purpose far greater than any temporary escape or earthly pleasure.

Like the swimmer struggling to stay afloat before reaching for the lifeline, we often face periods of doubt, frustration, and pain both before and after accepting God's hand. These feelings are a natural state of our human experience. Rather than being held hostage and incapacitated by these emotions, we can choose to accept and embrace them. Each moment of suffering then becomes an opportunity for change, molding us into stronger stewards of God's love. When we allow the LORD to work in the midst of our pain, we are led toward deeper healing and a closer relationship with him.

TRUSTING GOD'S PROCESS

Many times, we fail to recognize the lifeline God offers because we're too focused on our own plans. Often, we strive for control, believing that if we just try harder, things will improve. But just as a swimmer cannot be forced to take the lifeline, recovery cannot be imposed upon us—it's a personal decision that must come from within. When we feel pushed into sobriety, it often leads to resistance, resentment, and possibly relapse. Lasting change is sparked by either inspiration—an inner desire for a better life—or desperation, hitting rock bottom. In either case, the decision to get sober must come from within.

Transformation begins when we release our destructive plans and surrender to God's redemptive purpose for us. As we accept his hand, we may stumble or fall, but each mistake becomes a stepping stone on our journey to everlasting healing. The seeds of success are often planted in our failures, especially when we are resilient enough to rise again, learning and growing with each attempt.

As we walk the road to recovery, it's easy to become fixated on setbacks and failures. However, we must remember that every step—no matter how small—plays a part in God's greater work within us. Just as a swimmer must trust the lifeline, even when it feels uncomfortable or out of reach, we must trust that God's plan for us is perfect, even when the end result is unclear. And just as the swimmer must allow the rescuer to pull them to safety, we too must surrender to God, letting him guide us out of the turbulent currents of our dysfunction, even when we can't fully comprehend the depths of the waters we're trapped in.

The journey may be challenging, but it leads to continual growth and healing. Each step forward brings us closer to the redemption we deserve. When we let go of our definitions of success and failure—shaped by our timing and expectations—and embrace God's perfect timeline, we step into his presence, where serenity and contentment reside.

It is in this surrender to God's timing and plan that we often reach the pivotal moment—the turning point. It is here, when we are no longer bound by our past mistakes or the weight of our self-imposed limitations, that we find the courage to change. The moment we choose to trust in God's direction is the moment we step into a new reality—one where true transformation becomes possible.

REFLECTION QUESTIONS

1. Trusting God's Way: Are you still trying to save yourself, or are you ready to fully surrender and trust in God's way? What areas of your life are you holding on to, resisting his help, and how can you begin to let go and trust his plan for you?

2. Addiction, Failure, and Growth: How has your struggle with addiction and dependency shaped your view of failure and growth? How can you embrace your failures as essential steps in the learning process, knowing they contribute to your transformation and progress?

3. Learning from Mistakes: Are you open to learning from your mistakes, trusting that God is using them to refine you? How can you practice seeing each challenge as an opportunity to grow and trust in his refining process?

4. Reaching for the Lifeline: In which areas of your life do you need to stop resisting and begin trusting God's lifeline? How can you open your heart to his guidance on your path to recovery? Ask yourself: are you truly content living in dysfunction, or do you desire change? What would your life look like if you made decisions that aligned with God's will for you?

FAITH IN ACTION: THE CYCLE OF SELF-DESTRUCTION

Through consistent action and prayer, along with the support of a faith-filled community, you will grow closer to the person God has called you to be. Surrendering control, seeking his guidance, and trusting his process are the cornerstones of lasting change. You don't have to face this journey alone—God is with you, ready to carry you through the challenges and lead you toward the abundant life he has planned for you. Every step, no matter how small, is part of the greater journey of healing and restoration that God has in store for you. As you engage with these action points, you will begin to experience God's grace, which will lead you to lasting freedom and fulfillment.

1. Action Step: Surrender to God's Timing

   Begin each day by acknowledging that God's plan for your healing is greater than your own efforts. Pray for strength to trust his process and timing, especially during challenging moments.

   Why It Matters: Surrendering control opens the door for God's grace to work in you. Trusting his timing, even when it feels hard, leads to lasting transformation.

2. Action Step: Reflect on Your Identity in Christ

   Spend time reflecting on your true identity in Christ—loved, forgiven, and restored. Meditate on Scriptures such as Isa 55:7 and Ps 16:11 that remind you of God's promises and your worth in his eyes. If you'd prefer, find other passages that speak to you and inspire your curiosity to learn more about the great stories in the Bible.

   Why It Matters: Addiction distorts our sense of self-worth. Reclaiming your identity in Christ helps break the cycle of self-destruction and allows you to embrace healing.

3. Action Step: Engage in a Supportive Community

   Make it a priority to connect with a positive and supportive community, such as a faith-based group, a mentor, or trusted friends who encourage your recovery journey.

   Why It Matters: Addiction thrives in isolation. A supportive community provides accountability, encouragement, and shared strength to help you stay on track.

4. Action Step: Get a Bible and Study Guide

   Invest in a Bible study guide to help you understand the biblical stories on a deeper level. Ask a trusted pastor, priest, or someone familiar with the Bible for recommendations.

When selecting a Bible, choose a translation that speaks to you and is accessible.

Personal Reflection: I have several translations of the Bible, each speaking to me in unique ways. My primary Bible is tattered—many pages are dog-eared, written on, and some are even falling out. I've covered it with Post-it notes, marking passages that have resonated with me over the years, along with dates showing when I've read, reread, and revisited them. It's my trusted companion, offering countless hours of joy and helping me unlock the timeless, hidden wisdom that can only be found in the Scriptures. My study guide has been invaluable, shedding light on parts of the Bible that I would struggle to understand on my own. It has inspired me to explore additional resources, deepening my understanding. I find it exciting to dive into history to better grasp the context of Scripture and see how everything ties together.

Through my journey of faith and deeper understanding of the Scriptures, I've had the privilege of being invited to say the invocation at city council meetings from time to time. While my responsibilities for the city are highly technical and complex, being able to express my faith through prayer publicly at those meetings has been profoundly meaningful to me.

Why It Matters: A study guide helps you navigate difficult concepts and understand the context of ancient societal norms. The right Bible translation brings the stories to life and keeps your interest alive. It's OK to use different translations—just make sure you're doing your research. Translations range from simple reading levels to those preferred by theologians, and you never know where your newfound studies will take you, as evidenced with me.

As you take each step toward surrender, reflection, and community, trust that God's grace is guiding you toward healing and transformation. The actions you take—no matter how small—are part of his greater plan for your restoration. Stay committed to surrendering control, embracing your identity in Christ, and seeking support from others. Through these steps, God will lead you to lasting freedom and fulfillment.

3

The Turning Point

MUCH LIKE THE ISRAELITES who wandered for forty years in the wilderness after God freed them from enslavement by the Egyptians (as described in the book of Exodus and several subsequent chapters in the Old Testament), those of us trapped by addiction often find ourselves lost in a barren desert of confusion, isolation, and despair. Though we yearn for a release from our situation, the relentless cycle of addiction often makes escape seem impossible. Yet, just as God guided his people through the wilderness with unwavering faithfulness, he offers us the same divine guidance as we navigate the desolate landscape of addiction and dependency.

In our darkest moments, we may feel as though we are drifting aimlessly without purpose or direction. We chase hollow highs and temporary pleasures, hoping they will offer the serenity we crave or provide an escape from the pain that gnaws at our souls. But it's in these very moments of being lost—these times of weakness and desperation—that we begin to see the truth: authentic freedom is not found in substances but in the loving arms of God.

The Israelites' journey to the promised land was anything but easy. They faced trials, setbacks, and frustrations, much like we do in our recovery journey. Yet, through every challenge, God remained with them, guiding them through the wilderness. Similarly, God is with us—right in the midst of our struggles, walking alongside us through every step of recovery. He doesn't simply lead us out of the wilderness; he carries us through our trials and into the fulfillment of his promises. Just as God provided for the Israelites in the desert, he, too, provides for us.

THE FOG OF DESPAIR

In the depths of imprisonment, we live in a fog. This haze clouds our perception, distorting our sense of reality and leaving us disoriented, unable to see the truth about ourselves or the world around us. We become ensnared in cycles of justification, convincing ourselves that we'll stop tomorrow or that just one more time won't hurt.

Yet, in the quiet of our darkest times—when we can no longer hide from the truth—that voice we've heard over the years begins to pierce through the fog. It is not a voice of condemnation but a gentle whisper, calling us home: "Come to me, all who labor and are heavy laden, and I will give you rest" (Matt 11:28). At first, this whisper may seem soft, even imperceptible, but it is an invitation to surrender—to let go of control and allow Jesus to lead us out of desolation and into the rest only he can provide.

Just as the Israelites trusted God to lead them into the unknown, we, too, must place our trust in his guidance. In our dysfunctional state, we may have tried to unsuccessfully control every aspect of our lives, but choosing recovery means surrendering that control and opening ourselves to the LORD's transformative power. It is through this surrender that healing starts to take root as we are emancipated from our brokenness. This is an essential step on our journey, one that cannot be overlooked.

THE PATH TO REDEMPTION

The path to recovery often feels long and fraught with obstacles. Addiction may have stolen so much of our hope that we begin to question whether redemption is even possible or if life is worth living. Yet, no matter how far we've wandered, no matter how deeply our struggles have taken root in our lives, redemption is always within reach. "If we confess our sins, he is faithful and just, and will forgive our sins and cleanse us from all unrighteousness" (1 John 1:9).

God's grace is not limited by our mistakes or failures; his love reaches deeper than the scars left by addiction. Redemption is not a distant dream—it is a present reality that we begin to experience the moment we allow him to forgive us and cleanse us from the consequences of our past choices. In his mercy, we are given the opportunity to start anew, free from the weight of our past and empowered to walk forward in his love. As we read in Hos 6:3, "Let us know, let us press on to know the LORD; his going forth is sure as the dawn; he will come to us as the showers, as the spring rains that water the earth."

God's grace is like the gentle rains that restore the earth—nurturing, healing, and reviving the soul. As we take those first steps in recovery, we begin to realize that we are no longer captive to our desires and impulses.

EMBRACING THE NEW CREATION

The turning point in our spiritual journey is a pivotal moment—a time when we look back and recognize that every hardship, failure, and struggle we've faced has led us to this point: the complete submission of ourselves to God. We step away from the path of self-reliance and our attempts to fix ourselves, opening our hearts to the work only God can do. It is a season of yielding—letting go of the person we once were and embracing the new identity God has prepared for us.

At first, the trek may feel overwhelming, and the burdens of our past may seem insurmountable. But as we move forward, we realize that God is not merely cleaning us up—he is remaking us into something entirely new. As Paul writes in 2 Cor 5:17: "Therefore, if any one is in Christ, he is a new creation; the old has passed away, behold, the new has come." In Christ, the old has passed, and the new has joyfully arrived. Jesus is recreating us from the inside out, shaping a new life that reflects his glory, grace, and love.

Our renewal involves the intensive work of the LORD, reshaping the very essence of who we are—both internally and externally. Our desires are realigned with God's, our hearts softened to his will, and our minds renewed by his truth. We no longer live for the temporary pleasures of the world but for the eternal delight that comes from being in harmonious union with our Creator.

EXPERIENCING TRUE FREEDOM

As we step into our new identity in Christ, we begin to experience a freedom unlike anything we've known before. This freedom is not merely the absence of the chains of addiction or shame; it is the active presence of God's Spirit within us, guiding us along paths of tranquility. We grow confident—not in our own strength but in the power of knowing we are aligned with God's will. Our identity is no longer defined by past mistakes, addictions, or the lies we once believed about ourselves. We realize that we are now strengthened through Christ. As a result, when adversity strikes, suppression becomes impossible; instead, it strengthens us, because the foundation of our freedom is firmly established in the LORD.

This is the power of the turning point—it marks the beginning of a profound rebirth at the deepest level of our being. It's a spiritual revival that alters the course of our lives forever. We begin to see ourselves through God's eyes, recognizing our potential, worth, and the boundless love he has poured into us. We start walking in the fullness of who God has called us to be, confident in his love and empowered by his Spirit.

THE JOY OF GOD'S PRESENCE

As we continue our journey, something striking begins to unfold: we realize that the joy we once sought in substances can actually be found in the presence of God. Psalm 84:10 reminds us, "For a day in your courts is better than a thousand elsewhere. I would rather be a doorkeeper in the house of my God than dwell in the tents of wickedness." This verse speaks to the deep longing for true peace— a peace that surpasses the momentary relief substances offer. The temporary pleasures of drugs and alcohol pale in comparison to the serenity found in God's presence.

Addiction deceives us into believing that substances are needed to feel alive, but the truth is, we were designed to find life in God alone. True fulfillment is not sourced externally but in the LORD's love, which fully satisfies and restores our souls. As we spend time in his presence, we begin to experience a peace and contentment that far surpasses anything we could have known during our days of active use, when we were outside his house.

Even on the most challenging days of recovery—when we feel weak or tempted—we can draw strength from the joy of God's presence as we dwell in his courts. The world offers countless distractions, but nothing compares to the bliss that only God can provide.

STEPPING INTO THE SANCTUARY OF RECOVERY

Recovery can be best described as stepping out of the firestorm of addiction and dysfunction and into the peaceful sanctuary of God's grace. In his presence, we are renewed and restored. In his shelter, we finally find rest for our weary souls.

Surrendering to God means acknowledging that we cannot walk this path alone. We let go of our need to control the outcome and trust that God has a plan for our healing. As the prophet Jeremiah proclaims, "For I know the plans I have for you, says the LORD, plans for welfare and not for evil, to give you a future and a hope" (Jer 29:11). God's plan for our recovery exceeds anything we could design on our own. It may not always align with our expectations, but it will lead to a fulfillment far greater than the destructive path we once followed.

TRUSTING GOD'S PLAN FOR US

Trying to regain control of our lives on our own is an exercise in futility. However, trusting in God's will—and recognizing that his plan is far greater than anything we could have imagined for ourselves—is one of the most profound discoveries of our lives. We may feel as though we've wasted years wandering through a desert, but God is not confined by time. He has the power to redeem every moment, and his restoration unfolds perfectly, aligned with the unique rhythm of our circumstances.

In John 14:1–4, Christ reassures us:

> Let not your hearts be troubled; believe in God, believe also in me. In my Father's house are many rooms; if it were not so, would I have told you that I go to prepare a place for you? And when I go and prepare a place for you, I will come again and will take you to myself, that where I am you may be also. And you know the way where I am going.

In God's house, there is always room for us. Each room is uniquely designed to meet our individual needs, address our specific struggles, and celebrate our distinct gifts. It is a place of peace, rest, and healing, where we are never turned away.

The journey of recovery is one of profound change. While it may not always be easy, it is the path to everlasting freedom. As we surrender our old plans and trust in God's purpose for us, we step into a life filled with hope and the joy of his presence as he restores us into a new person.

As we continue to surrender, old habits are not just left behind; we are being remade, reshaped into the people we were always meant to be. This gradual process of renewal touches every aspect of our lives, transforming us into a new creation with each passing day.

REFLECTION QUESTIONS

1. Acknowledging Addiction's Hold: In what ways has addiction kept you captive? What intentional steps can you take to break free from the chains you've placed on yourself? Have you tried to get sober before but struggled to stay clean? If so, what led to your relapse?

2. Ready to Listen—Surrendering to God's Guidance: Are you ready to stop running from God and listen to his gentle whisper? How can you open your heart to hear his voice more clearly?

3. Trusting God More Fully in Recovery: In what areas of your recovery can you trust God more fully? Are there still areas where you're holding back from surrendering to him? If so, why?

4. Surrendering Your Plan for God's Better Plan: Are you truly willing to let God into your life? How can you trust that his plan will lead you to deeper freedom and lasting peace? Are you ready to take a leap of faith, even without knowing his plan for you?

FAITH IN ACTION: THE TURNING POINT

Your journey is shaped by key turning points—moments where your faith moves beyond passive belief into active surrender. The following action steps are designed to guide you through these critical moments, helping you embrace God's will while trusting in his process. Each turning point presents a chance to live out your faith more deeply, stepping into the healing that God has in store for you. With every action, you open the door for transformation, trusting that God is at work in every step of your recovery.

1. Surrender Your Control
   - Action Step: The Israelites' journey through the wilderness was defined by surrender—letting go of control and

trusting God's guidance. In the same way, your recovery requires a deep surrender to God's will. Take a moment today to acknowledge the areas where you've been trying to control your life or your recovery. In prayer, submit those areas to God, trusting that his plan is greater than your own. Ask him to guide your steps, knowing that your surrender opens the door for lasting change.

- Personal Reflection: I ended up Baker Acted in a mental facility, completely out of my mind and overdosed on a cocktail of drugs. After I sobered up and began to understand the full impact of my situation, I realized that if I continued on the path I was on, I would be dead soon. It was then that I literally got on my knees while my schizophrenic roommate was having a tantrum and asked for deliverance as I gave my life over to the LORD. I could not handle my life any longer. My life has not been the same since!

- Why It Matters: Just as the Israelites had to release their desire for control to experience God's guidance in the wilderness, your recovery requires the same surrender. When you hold on too tightly, you limit God's ability to move in your life. Yielding to God opens the door to his transformative power, allowing him to lead you with wisdom and strength. Trusting God with your recovery process allows you to experience life in ways you couldn't achieve through your own efforts.

2. Embrace the Process of Renewal

- Action Step: As God led the Israelites step-by-step, he is guiding you through the process of recovery. It may feel long, full of obstacles, and even overwhelming, but each step is a step toward healing. Recognize that God is not just fixing you—he is remaking you. Reflect on the areas of your life where God has already begun to initiate renewal. If it's hard to identify any change, remember you are reading this book—that's a sign of God at work in you! Identify one specific area where you can embrace his transforming power and take a step forward in faith.

- Why It Matters: God doesn't just fix you; he remakes you. This renewal process might feel long or difficult at times, but each step forward is progress toward healing and spiritual growth. Give God time to work in you. When you embrace the journey, you deepen your relationship with God, trusting his timing and perfect work. Acknowledging and actively participating in this process allows you to experience a fuller and richer life in Christ, prepared for the challenges ahead.

3. Find Rest in God's Presence

- Recovery is not just about stopping old behaviors but finding true rest and fulfillment in God's presence. Reflect on Ps 84:10 or other psalms that speak to you. Take intentional time today to seek God's presence, whether through prayer, reading Scripture, or simply sitting in stillness. Let his peace fill your heart and remind you that true rest is found in him, not in the temporary highs or distractions of addiction.

- Why It Matters: Recovery is more than just quitting old behaviors; it's about finding fulfillment and peace in God. Addiction leaves you empty, but true rest and restoration come from God's presence alone. By choosing to spend time with him and investing in your relationship with him, you allow his peace to quiet your anxious heart and rejuvenate your spirit, enabling you to face the challenges of recovery with renewed strength and clarity.

4. Trust in God's Plan for Your Future

- Action Step: As you step into the sanctuary of recovery, trust that God's plan for your healing is far greater than what you could design for yourself. Take a moment to pray over Jer 29:11, which reminds you that God has a plan for your welfare, not for harm but to give you a future filled with hope. In your prayer, commit to trusting God's timing and plan for your recovery, even when it feels uncertain or stagnant. Trust that every step you take is part of his redemptive work in your life.

- Why It Matters: Recovery can sometimes feel uncertain, but God's plans are always good, filled with hope and promise. When you trust in his perfect timing and divine wisdom, you surrender your need for control and open yourself to the fulfillment of his purposes. Trusting his plan brings peace, knowing that he is at work even in moments of difficulty or frustration and that his redemptive work in your life will ultimately bring about your flourishing.

5. Celebrate the Joy of Freedom

- Action Step: The turning point in recovery is not just about overcoming addiction—it's about experiencing the bliss that comes from walking in alignment with God's will. Reflect on the joy you can experience when you walk with God, and make a conscious effort to celebrate the victories, both big and small. Whether it's a day of sobriety, a renewed sense of peace, or simply a moment of clarity, take time to give thanks to God for the freedom he is giving you. This is the joy that the world cannot offer.

- Why It Matters: Recovery is about stepping into the freedom that God offers. This joy is a deep, lasting peace that transcends worldly pleasures. By celebrating these victories, you acknowledge God's work in your life, strengthening your faith and encouraging continued growth.

By embracing these action points, you are taking deliberate steps toward the healing and growth God has planned for you. Each action is not only a tool for recovery but also a way to deepen your faith and experience God's presence and power in your life. As you surrender, embrace, rest, trust, and celebrate, you will grow in your relationship with him and find liberation from your past.

4

The Remake

TRANSFORMATION IS AN ONGOING, deeply spiritual journey in which we allow God to rebuild us. Through this process, we discover authentic freedom—not through our own strength or willpower but through surrendering to the life-giving guidance of the Holy Spirit. As Jesus discussed with his followers in John 6:63, "It is the Spirit that gives life, the flesh is of no avail; the words that I have spoken to you are Spirit and life." These words remind us that true life comes from the Spirit, not from gratifying the flesh or pursuing worldly endeavors.

When we open ourselves to be remade, we are invited to release the old, decaying parts of our lives—addictions, dependencies, toxic relationships, and mindsets that no longer serve us. Instead, we are called to embrace the abundant life that Christ offers through his bread of eternal life. This process can feel unsettling, as change often does. However, just as Jesus spoke to his followers in the "bread of life" discourse found in John 6, we too are invited to choose the everlasting life that Christ offers through his body and blood. For those willing to surrender and follow Jesus, redemption becomes possible because he is the true bread of life.

THE POWER OF THE HOLY SPIRIT
IN TRANSFORMATION

It is the Holy Spirit who breathes life into our weary souls, offering renewal and empowering us to walk in victory. Recovery is not just about stopping harmful behaviors—because, on our own, we cannot always do that. Instead, it is about fully submitting to the LORD and allowing the Spirit to work in and through us, initiating lasting change.

We're bound to feel as though we're in a state of upheaval during the initial stages of our transformation. But much like an old home being gutted and then prepared for renovation, when placed in the hands of the master carpenter, our brokenness becomes the foundation for his glorious reconstruction. Trusting his methods and allowing him to work within us is key. While this process can feel uncomfortable at first, it's a necessary step that prepares us for the new life ahead and sets the stage for significant growth. This "stripping away" clears the path for greater freedom, deeper understanding, and a closer relationship with God. Above all, it's essential to remain open to his guidance so he can accomplish the work he desires in us.

We continue our journey with God when we intentionally set aside quiet time to be with him, patiently awaiting his guidance. God speaks to us in many ways, but it can be difficult to hear his voice amid the anxieties of daily life. That's why uninterrupted personal time with God is so essential. When we learn to simply be in his presence, the concerns of the world lose their urgency and power over us.

One of the biggest challenges in our modern, perpetually plugged-in world is overcoming the constant stream of distractions that demand our attention. However, as we master the art of quieting the noise, we grant ourselves the opportunity to be more aware of the Spirit's presence within us. When we free our minds, our body and soul follow—even if only for a moment—allowing us to experience something deeper than our human existence. Once we feel this with the full array of our senses, we'll continually yearn for more.

THE REMAKING PROCESS: TRUSTING
THE MASTER CARPENTER

As we embrace these changes, we should understand that it won't always be neat or easy. God doesn't rush the process of remaking us, nor does he cut corners. He is patient, methodical, and precise—a master carpenter carefully crafting something beautiful from our raw and imperfect materials.

The old patterns of thinking, living, and acting are deeply ingrained in us, so they won't vanish overnight. Our repressed pain also needs healing—not through substances, as we did in the past, but through God's love. With his guidance—through prayer, reflection, Scripture, and the Holy Spirit—the pieces of our new life will gradually begin to fall into place. At first, the changes may seem small and almost imperceptible, but over time, we'll notice how different aspects of our life begin to align. Much like an incomplete puzzle that once seemed confusing, we'll start to see improvements in areas that previously held us back. What felt unclear will eventually become as obvious as a newly placed piece in the puzzle.

Our attitude is crucial. Viewing the glass as half full rather than half empty helps us maintain optimism—even when faced with challenging interactions or situations with family, friends, co-workers, or strangers. Staying positive also allows us to better recognize the areas in our lives that need improvement as the LORD reveals them to us and guides us on how to make those changes. As we follow his direction, we'll begin making decisions that align with our newfound identity in Christ—choices that honor God and reflect the changes taking place within us.

Ephesians 2:19-20 reminds us: "So then you are no longer strangers and sojourners, but you are fellow citizens with the saints and members of the household of God, built upon the foundation of the apostles and prophets, Christ Jesus himself being the cornerstone." Just as Paul wrote to the people of Ephesus many years ago, the foundation of our new identity today is built on Christ as the cornerstone. As we place our trust in him, we can be confident that the process of change—though sometimes unpleasant—is always for our good.

CUTTING TIES WITH THE OLD

One of the most challenging aspects of recovery is letting go of old patterns, unhealthy relationships, and memories that keep us tethered to our past. These were once sources of false comfort or a distorted sense of identity but now burden us as we are remade. In 1 Pet 4, Peter writes about Christian restraint and being good stewards of God's grace, urging us to recognize that our past indulgences—whether in substances, behaviors, or relationships—no longer serve us. They stand in opposition to the new creation that God is shaping us to become.

This process of severing ties with the past can be awkward and painful. Former friends or family members may misunderstand our choices, question our decisions, or even try to lure us back into old habits. They might slander us or ridicule our newfound convictions. But we should remember that these old attachments no longer align with the life we are now called to live. As we embrace our new identity in Christ, we're not walking away because we have outgrown others but because we are growing into something new, led by God's direction.

Our true family is found in the body of Christ—among those who have also been made new through God's love. In this new family, we find support, encouragement, and accountability. We must fiercely protect our recovery, guarding our hearts and minds against the distractions that seek to pull us back into the old patterns of addiction.

THE INNER-DOBERMAN:
GUARDING OUR SOBRIETY

In all stages of recovery, sobriety is a precious treasure that must be fiercely protected. We can tap into our "inner-Doberman," a vigilant guardian of our newfound freedom to help us. Just as a Doberman guards its master with loyalty, courage, and strength, we can protect our sobriety with similar passion, guarding it against the temptations and pressures that could derail our progress.

This means setting firm boundaries—whether distancing ourselves from certain people, or avoiding situations that reignite old patterns. It also requires being proactive in safeguarding our spiritual, mental, and emotional health. Our "inner-Doberman" is not passive but active, alert, and disciplined, always on guard to protect the priceless gift of sobriety. This may involve taking assertive actions, like learning to say *no*, walking away from triggers, or seeking help when needed.

A NEW IDENTITY: WALKING IN CONFIDENCE

As we grow in our walk with the LORD, we begin to notice the signs of change. We make better decisions—not out of obligation or coercion but because our new identity in Christ is becoming who we really are. The cravings and desires that once controlled us—the need for substances, unhealthy relationships, or temporary pleasures—no longer have power over us. Instead, we begin to hunger and thirst for what is right in God's eyes, for the life that comes from living in alignment with his will.

This is the power of the transformation we are experiencing. No longer driven by fear, impulses, or self-doubt, we are led by the Spirit, walking confidently in the truth of who we are in Christ. Our confidence is rooted in a deep, abiding trust in God's provision to see us through all difficulties.

TESTING AND REFINING: GROWING
STRONG THROUGH TRIALS

Pain and suffering, though we often fear and try to avoid, have the power to elevate us to the next level in our spiritual growth. They become tools in God's hands to refine us, to deepen our trust in him, and to bring us closer to the image of Christ. When we embrace the lessons that come with hardship rather than resisting them, we open ourselves to the Holy Spirit's work. Ultimately, through these trials, we grow stronger, more resilient, and more deeply grounded in God's love and purpose. As Paul tells us in Romans, "More than that, we rejoice in our sufferings, knowing that suffering produces endurance, and endurance produces character, and character produces hope" (Rom 5:3-4). Through our trials, we develop endurance that strengthens our hope in God's promise of salvation.

In Hebrews, the author bolsters their argument by quoting from Proverbs in discussing the virtues of accepting trials as discipline and as a teaching instrument from the LORD: "And have you forgotten the exhortation which addresses you as sons?—'My son, do not regard lightly the discipline of the Lord, nor lose courage when you are punished by him. For the Lord disciplines him whom he loves, and chastises every son whom he receives'" (Heb 12:5-6).

As we embrace our new identity in Christ, God will continue to groom us through trials. These acts are not out of anger, but rather out of love. Tribulations are essential for our growth. The discipline we're developing ensures that we are prepared to face these challenges. While these trials may feel difficult and at times painful, they are a vital part of our spiritual journey.

As James reminds us, "Count it all joy, my brethren, when you meet various trials, for you know that the testing of your faith produces steadfastness. And let steadfastness have its full effect, that you may be perfect and complete, lacking in nothing" (Jas 1:2-4). Through these tests, our faith is refined and strengthened, and we become better prepared to reach the next level in our spiritual walk.

Though trials can be difficult and exhausting, they offer us a valuable opportunity to shift our perspective. Pain and suffering, instead of being viewed through the lens of fear and dread, can be seen as signs of growth and spiritual development. In the midst of challenging times, we should seek to understand the lessons God may be teaching us through his discipline. While not every trial is a form of discipline from God, as we grow closer to him, we develop the discernment to recognize the difference. This growing ability to discern allows us to distinguish between trials that are refining us and those that are simply part of the human experience.

Regardless of the source of our suffering, we always have a choice: we can either let our trials hold us back, or we can use them as motivation to move forward on our journey. Instead of viewing them through a lens of discouragement and disappointment, we can choose to see our tribulations as opportunities to strengthen our resolve and deepen our steadfastness. By making this choice, we refuse to be overcome or derailed by our circumstances. Instead, we trust that God is using each situation to build us up, drawing us closer to the person he's calling us to be.

Jesus himself was not exempt from suffering during his time on earth. Therefore, following the LORD doesn't promise a life free from hardship, but it assures us that he walks alongside us every step of the way, fully understanding our struggles. His example shows us that suffering is not the end of the story, but rather a vital part of our journey—one that leads to growth, deeper purpose, and a closer relationship with God.

SURRENDERING ANGER

At times, we can feel overwhelmed by pain, resentment, or despair when facing trials. When we hold on to these emotions for too long, anger can take root. And when we cling to anger, it can strain our relationship with our heavenly Father. As Paul wisely advises in Eph 4:26, "Be angry but do not sin; do not let the sun go down on your anger." While emotions like pain, resentment, and anger are natural aspects of the human experience, if left unresolved, they can hinder our communication with God. These unresolved feelings create a thick barrier, making it difficult to hear God's voice or recognize his work in our lives.

In times of suffering, we are never alone. God's presence is just as real in our sorrow as it is in our joy. When we surrender our pain and anger to him during our trials, he melts our bitterness as if it were ice dissolving in warm water. By doing so, we keep ourselves open to his love, which purifies us and creates space for continued healing and grace.

THE ONGOING JOURNEY

We should keep in mind that our remake is not a destination; it's just the beginning. While it marks a profound change, it's the start of a new chapter in our rebirth. We will still face challenges. We will still experience pain. We will still get angry. We will continue to encounter trials that test our faith and endurance. But the difference now is that we face these obstacles from a place of strength, firmly planted in the truth that we are new creations in Christ. We no longer fight these battles alone; we fight them with God's power within us. We walk in his grace, led by his Spirit, and live in the victory that Christ has already won for us.

The road ahead may be challenging at times, but it is filled with hope. The pain we experience has purpose—God uses it to refine us and draw us closer to the person he has called us to be. Every struggle and trial becomes an opportunity to lean more fully into God's grace, trusting that he is working everything for our good. As we endure, we grow in fortitude. As we face temptation, we become more resilient. As we experience trials, our faith is strengthened.

In Romans, Paul reminds us that "we know that in everything God works for good with those who love him, who are called according to his purpose" (Rom 8:28). Even in our suffering, we can trust that God is working in us and through us for our good. The challenges we face are not punishment or signs of failure; they are part of the process of being remade. We are being reshaped into the person God has always known we could be.

TRUSTING GOD'S PLAN

As we continue on our journey, we can rest in the assurance that God is not finished with us. The pain and challenges we encounter are guiding us toward something greater. Our trials are not the end of the story—they are the very means by which God is drawing us into a deeper, more intimate relationship with him.

Trials and tribulations, when surrendered to God, become powerful agents of transformation. It is in the furnace of suffering that God refines and molds us into stronger, more resilient individuals—those no longer weighed down by the chains of addiction but who rise as warriors for his kingdom.

Every moment of suffering, doubt, and struggle is an opportunity for God to work within us. As we endure, we will look back and realize that the season when we surrendered to God—when we allowed him to begin remaking us—was the turning point that transformed everything in our beautiful new life.

We are no longer the people we once were. We are new creations in the LORD, and the best is yet to come. Let us continue to press forward with confidence, knowing that God is faithful to complete the work he has begun in us. Let us embrace the transformation process, trusting that he is leading us to a place of freedom, wholeness, and accountability in him.

As we continue on this journey, it's essential that we remain grounded in honesty—both with ourselves and with others. Freedom is not simply a destination; it is built on the foundation of being real about where we are, what we've faced, and the steps we still need to take. Embracing truth and accountability allows us to fully walk in the freedom Christ has promised without hiding behind masks or pretending to be something we're not.

REFLECTION QUESTIONS

1. Embracing the Process of Transformation: How do you respond to the difficult or painful times in your recovery? Do you view them as essential for your spiritual and personal growth, or do you find yourself resisting them? How can you adjust your perspective to see these challenges as opportunities for deeper transformation and greater change?

2. Guarding Your Sobriety: In what areas of your life do you need to set firmer boundaries to safeguard your recovery? Are there relationships or situations that are drawing you back into old habits, and how can you create healthier patterns that reflect your new identity in Christ?

3. Finding Confidence in Your New Identity: As you experience transformation, what are the initial signs that you're living more in alignment with your new identity in Christ? How can you build greater confidence in making decisions from a place of faith rather than fear or old patterns of addiction?

FAITH IN ACTION: THE REMAKE

Transformation is an ongoing journey where you allow God to reshape you. As you walk through this process, there are practical action steps you can take to remain open to his work in your life. These steps help you guard your newfound freedom and grow in your identity in Christ. While the remaking process can feel challenging at first, each step is an opportunity for you to embrace the change God is bringing about in you.

1. Embrace Quiet Time

   - Action Step: Set aside fifteen to thirty minutes each day to be still before God. Turn off distractions (especially your phone), focus solely on his presence, and invite the Holy Spirit to guide you in your transformation.

   - Why It Matters: Quiet time is essential for spiritual growth. It creates space for you to hear from God, receive renewal, and grow in understanding, strength, and grace.

2. Sever Old Ties

   - Action Step: Identify areas where old patterns, behaviors, or relationships are holding you back. Ask God for the strength to cut these ties and make room for the new identity he is creating in you.

- Why It Matters: Letting go of past influences allows you to embrace the new life God has planned for you. Breaking free from old ties is essential for embracing change and walking in freedom.

3. Guard Your Sobriety

  - Action Step: Take proactive steps to protect the changes you've made. Identify situations or people that threaten your peace and set boundaries to safeguard your recovery and new life.

  - Personal Reflection: I never truly understood the value of saying *no* until I embraced my gift of sobriety. Saying *no* isn't just about setting boundaries with others—it's also about saying *no* to myself. Self-denial has been essential for building my character, and learning to say *no* has become a powerful tool in guarding my peace. My "inner-Doberman" helps me in this process—this fierce, protective side of me that stands guard and ensures I stay focused on what's truly important. One practice that's been particularly helpful for me is distilling situations down to black and white. If I don't do this, I allow gray areas to open the door for ambiguity to creep in. And in recovery, ambiguity and sobriety don't mix. I've lost some people along the way by learning to say *no*, but I've come to understand that it's OK. Prioritizing my sobriety and peace has been worth it.

  - Why It Matters: Guarding your sobriety ensures a strong foundation for your recovery. Boundaries protect your progress, helping you stay grounded in the transformation God is doing within you.

4. Embrace the Struggles

  - Action Step: When faced with trials or temptations, remember that these challenges are opportunities for growth. Trust that God is refining you through them and shaping you into the person he is calling you to be.

- Why It Matters: Struggles are opportunities for growth, not failure. Embracing them deepens your trust in God and prepares you for the fullness of his purpose in your life.

5. Be Real and Honest

- Action Step: Be honest with yourself and others about your struggles and progress. Honesty can be intimidating and scary at first, but once you practice, it will become second nature. Embrace the freedom that comes with authenticity and commit to walking in the freedom Christ has promised. Today, tell a trusted friend one thing that they do not know about you—something you've kept hidden and no one else knows.

- Why It Matters: Being real and honest invites deeper healing and freedom. Transparency with God and others cultivates trust and growth, making it easier to walk in the freedom Christ offers. Small acts of honesty lead to greater freedom from your past.

By walking these steps in faith, you allow God to continue working in your life, guiding you toward a life of greater freedom, peace, and purpose. Keep trusting in his plan, knowing that you are becoming the person he created you to be. Honesty with others fosters a reciprocal pattern of vulnerability, inspiring confidence and building trust in relationships. Remember, the friends you surround yourself with are a direct reflection of who you are.

5

Keeping It Real

IN THE EARLY STAGES of recovery, one of the most crucial steps is taking responsibility for our actions. The weight of self-doubt and uncertainty can often feel overwhelming, but it's through embracing the truth that we begin to break free from these fears. A key to our renewal is "keeping it real"—being honest with ourselves, others, and God.

This foundation of honesty begins with a reflection on our past, a vigilant awareness of our present state, and a strong commitment to living in truth as we move forward. By embracing truth, we invite the Holy Spirit to guide us through setbacks and challenges. Through our obstacles, we can find comfort in knowing that God's love for us is rooted in our very imperfection. It is in accepting his love—with all our flaws—that we discover the true freedom we seek as we embrace our identity as children of God.

LIVING IN TRUTH, LETTING GO OF LIES

Recovery requires a shift in how we see ourselves and the world around us. No longer can we blame others or external circumstances for our struggles. When we point fingers, we live a lie. The biggest lie we can believe is that the source of our troubles lies outside of us when, in truth, the battles we face often begin from within. This lie spawns more lies, entangling us further in a web of deception. In our attempts to protect ourselves, we deepen our disconnection from the truth. Yet, only by abandoning these lies can we experience the freedom that comes with embracing the truth of our situation. Anything less than honest acknowledgment of the extent of our problems may lead us back to Egypt—back to personal enslavement.

Psalm 103:2–5 beautifully illustrates God's mercy and healing:

> Bless the LORD, O my soul, and forget not all his benefits, who forgives all your iniquity, who heals all your diseases, who redeems your life from the Pit, who crowns you with mercy and compassion, who satisfies you with good as long as you live so that your youth is renewed like the eagle's.

When God lifts us from the pit we've dug for ourselves by healing us from the disease of addiction, he also crowns us with mercy. Living honestly with both ourselves and God opens us to his healing and redemptive power. Moreover, being honest with those around us continues that healing process. True recovery isn't just about us; it's about sharing our newfound freedom with others, helping them rise from their pit as well.

Being honest isn't always comfortable. It's often painful as it forces us to confront the most difficult parts of ourselves. But when we choose to walk in the light and embrace the truth—no matter how uncomfortable—it draws us closer to the LORD. God is the truth, and when we live in his true light, we continue to experience transformation. From the depths of our past, we can rise and soar like an eagle, crowned not with shame, as we once were, but with the mercy of God. His grace lifts us from the darkness into the light, transforming our wounds into a testimony of his redemptive love and power. With every step forward, we are renewed, reminded that no matter how far we've fallen, his mercy is always greater.

BECOMING SOLDIERS OF FAITH

In Mark 7, Jesus rebukes those who honor him only with their lips yet fail to honor him in their hearts. True worship is not about what we say—it's about how we live. Christ calls us to be warriors of faith, not simply talkers but doers. This is because the kingdom of heaven does not advance through passive observation but through active, passionate commitment.

Jesus tells us in the book of Matthew, "From the days of John the Baptist until now the kingdom of heaven has suffered violence, and men of violence take it by force. For all the prophets and the law prophesied until John; and if you are willing to accept it, he is Eli'jah who is to come" (Matt 11:12–14). This is not a call to physical violence but to spiritual violence—an unshakable, fierce commitment to pursue God's will, no matter the cost.

As addicts, we are no strangers to extremes. Driven by passion and intensity, we often find ourselves trapped in self-destructive behaviors. But what if we channeled this powerful energy into something greater? What if we became warriors of faith, living with the same fervor that Elijah did—who called fire down from heaven (see 2 Kgs 1:10–14) and ascended to heaven in a blazing chariot (see 2 Kgs 2:11)? Instead of surrendering to the destruction brought on by drugs, we can surrender to God's call, directing our intensity toward spiritual heroism and the pursuit of God's will. We can look to Elijah's life as an example for our own.

PATIENCE, PERSEVERANCE, AND DISCIPLINE

To truly take heaven by force, we must cultivate patience, perseverance, and discipline. These qualities form the foundation of spiritual strength in recovery. While each plays a distinct role, they work together to guide us through the most challenging moments. Patience and perseverance are what enable us to remain steadfast, even when the road feels never-ending. They give us the resolve to keep going despite setbacks, temptations, or feelings of failure. It's the quiet determination to move forward, one step at a time, trusting that freedom, peace, and redemption are worth every ounce of effort.

In Luke 8:15, Jesus speaks about cultivating patience with planting seeds in good soil as he explains the parable of the sower: "And as for that in the good soil, they are those who, hearing the word, hold it fast in an honest and good heart, and bring forth fruit with patience." Patience isn't passive; it's an active commitment to stay anchored in truth and allow God's word to bear fruit in our lives. It's a deep internal strength that empowers us to refuse to let circumstances disrupt our peace.

Patience and perseverance should be complemented with discipline, which is equally essential. Discipline is the ability to choose what is right over what feels comfortable or familiar. It's the strength to stay committed to the path of growth, even when it's challenging, and to make choices that align with our higher purpose rather than our immediate desires. Through discipline, we build resilience and cultivate the habits that lead to lasting transformation. Discipline means establishing boundaries, managing our time, and making decisions with intention. It's not about perfection; it's about commitment to the process, even on days when we don't feel like it. It's about showing up for ourselves, trusting that each small step forward adds up to meaningful progress in the long run.

Recovery doesn't promise immediate relief or instant results. The path is often rugged, and the struggles may feel overwhelming at times. Yet, it's through discipline—choosing daily to live in alignment with the truth, surrendering control, and staying true to our commitments—that we begin to build the momentum necessary for sustained growth. Discipline is rooted in self-control, a fruit of the Spirit, and it's essential for overcoming temptation and staying on track in recovery. With each day, as we exercise this self-control, we build strength and resilience, allowing us to face challenges with faith and determination.

As we cultivate discipline in small, everyday decisions, we begin to see the big changes that follow. It's through discipline—practiced with patience—that we develop the ability to endure hardship without giving in to frustration and stay focused on the purpose God has set for us, even in the hardest times. Second Timothy 1:7 reminds us "for God did not give us a spirit of timidity but a spirit of power and love and self-control." This divine empowerment enables us to practice the discipline needed for recovery, and in doing so, we experience spiritual growth and transformation. Each time we exercise discipline and self-control in recovery, we grow stronger and more aligned with God's will for our lives.

Discipline also involves taking ownership of our spiritual practices, which are essential for staying on track in recovery. This includes setting aside time for daily prayer, Scripture reading, attending worship services, and cultivating an active relationship with God. These practices help us connect with his presence, guiding our thoughts, words, and actions. And just as our recovery journey may not always feel exhilarating, there are times in our walk with the LORD when things may feel quiet or subdued. It's in these seasons that discipline keeps us grounded, helping us stay focused on the long-term goal. Even when progress feels slow, our routine provides the steady foundation that sustains us, reminding us that God is always at work—even in the quiet moments.

In times of struggle or doubt, it's easy to feel disconnected or believe that change is out of reach. But when practiced faithfully, discipline ensures that even on quiet, uneventful days, we are still making progress. It's the daily decisions we make, aligned with God's will, that gradually transform us. So, when the road feels long or difficult, we should remember that every moment of self-control—no matter how small—is shaping us into stronger, more resilient followers of Christ. Each choice may seem insignificant in the moment, but over time, they lead to profound growth, drawing us closer to the fullness of the life God has promised.

Together, patience, perseverance, and discipline form the armor we need to withstand the battle in recovery. By embracing these qualities, we begin to claim the freedom and peace God has promised us—one disciplined step at a time.

EMULATING ELIJAH

Ultimately, the goal of recovery is not merely to overcome addiction but to be transformed into vessels of God's power, purpose, and glory. Those of us who once found ourselves trapped in the depths of darkness now have the opportunity to rise with the same strength as Elijah, filled with the courage to take heaven by force, live with unshakable conviction, and advance the kingdom of God here on earth.

When we cultivate discipline and persevere with patience through trying times, we become soldiers of faith—individuals who have learned the deep value of endurance and courage in the face of adversity. We are no longer victims of our circumstances; we are passionate warriors for God's kingdom, advancing heaven on earth with boldness, passion, and perseverance.

When fully surrendered to God, our struggles no longer bind us but become the very tools that empower us to accomplish great spiritual feats. This is the radical call of recovery through Christ: not just to overcome addiction but to be transformed into the warriors God always intended us to be.

We are called to be fierce advocates and co-heirs of God's kingdom, using the newfound power he's given us to fight for his will. We prove that addiction does not define us—God's grace and power do. As we embrace our purpose with honesty and conviction, we step boldly into the mission of advancing heaven on earth, becoming mighty instruments of God's will. This mission is not just for ourselves but for others still lost in the wilderness, helping guide them toward the freedom and healing we've found in the LORD.

To live out this mission effectively, we must recognize that recovery is not a journey we walk alone. It is a shared experience, one that thrives within community. The healing we experience in Christ is meant to be extended to others as we walk alongside our fellow brothers and sisters in faith, supporting and uplifting one another. True recovery happens when we keep in mind our connection with others, and their mutual support creates a collective strength that propels us all forward in God's healing plan.

REFLECTION QUESTIONS

1. Recognizing God's Call and Redemption: Have you ever heard God's call, offering peace and guidance, even in the darkest moments of your addiction and struggles? How does his unwavering promise of redemption—no matter how far you've fallen—ignite hope in you and radically transform your understanding of recovery?

2. Being Honest: Do you fear being truly honest with yourself, God, or others? What are the barriers or fears holding you back from embracing full transparency? Take a moment to reflect on what you need to let go of in order to live with more authenticity. How can you take intentional steps to open your heart, be honest with yourself, and invite God into your healing process?

3. Emulating Elijah: How can you channel your energy to become more like Elijah, bold in faith and action? What fears are holding you back from being a warrior for God? How can you live more intentionally today, embracing the purpose God has for you and preparing for the day you meet him? Reflect on the steps you can take to live with courage, purpose, and faith, just like Elijah.

FAITH IN ACTION: KEEPING IT REAL

The journey of recovery is not just about overcoming obstacles but about embracing a deeper, authentic relationship with God. "Keeping it real" means being honest with yourself, cultivating spiritual discipline, and taking intentional steps toward lasting change. This section offers practical action steps to help you stay grounded as you move forward in your recovery. By committing to these actions, you align your daily choices with God's purpose, allowing his power to guide your healing and growth.

1. Honest Reflection: Write and Reflect

- Action Step: Begin by writing a letter to God or someone in your life. Be completely honest about your current struggles, fears, and hopes. Acknowledge the ways you've been hiding from the truth—whether it's avoiding responsibility, justifying past behaviors, or not being fully honest with yourself or others. Use this letter as a way to release your burdens and open yourself up to growth.

- Action Step: Reflect on Ps 103:2–5: In this reflection, express gratitude for God's mercy, and allow his healing grace to remind you that his love covers your imperfections. Recognize the depth of God's forgiveness, which is essential to embracing the truth about yourself.

- Personal Reflection: In my journey of recovery, one of the hardest but most healing steps I took was making amends with my family, whom I had hurt deeply during my active addiction years. I wrote a personal letter to each of them, outlining my shortcomings, failures, and sincere apologies. We gathered together as a family, and in that setting, I addressed each loved one individually, confessing my actions and the pain I had caused. My mother—whose quiet strength had always anchored us—looked at me with tearful eyes as I apologized for the sleepless nights and the worry I had brought her. My father—stoic and proud—nodded slowly as I admitted my mistakes and the disappointment I knew I had become. My sister—once my closest confidante—listened in silence as I acknowledged how I had let her down and strained the bond we once shared. My niece—wise beyond her years—met my eyes without flinching as I came clean with my deeds. It was nerve-racking and one of the most difficult things I've ever done, but it was also incredibly liberating. Confronting the truth of my mistakes and offering heartfelt apologies was an essential part of my healing process.

- Why It Matters: Honesty is key to healing and growth. Writing to God or others and reflecting on his mercy allows you to confront the truth about yourself and your journey, creating space for healing and deeper intimacy with God.

2. Daily Discipline: Commit to a Spiritual Practice

   - Action Step: Start your day with a moment of spiritual discipline. This can be a time of prayer, Scripture reading, or meditation. Use this time to focus on the truth of your recovery journey—both the struggles and the victories— and ask God to guide you through the day with patience, perseverance, and discipline.

   - Action Step: Consider setting specific, achievable goals for the day, such as reading a Bible verse, practicing a five-minute prayer, or journaling about your recovery progress. These small acts of discipline keep you grounded in the truth and help you grow spiritually.

   - Why It Matters: Consistent spiritual discipline helps you stay rooted in God's truth and strengthens your spiritual growth. It keeps you focused on his plan for your life and enables you to face each day with renewed strength and commitment.

3. Cultivate Patience: One Step at a Time

   - Action Step: When setbacks or temptations arise, remind yourself of the journey ahead. Patience is not about waiting passively; it's about staying grounded and taking one step at a time. Reflect on Luke 8:15 and how you can apply it to your life.

   - Action Step: This week, choose one area in your recovery where you need more patience (for example, with yourself, your progress, or dealing with external challenges). Commit to practicing patience in this area, trusting that growth is happening beneath the surface.

- Why It Matters: Patience helps you endure the inevitable challenges of recovery with grace. It encourages you to trust that God's timing is perfect, even when you can't see the full picture, and it enables you to grow steadily and persistently.

4. Community Support: Share Your Truth

- Action Step: Recovery is not a solitary journey. Seek out a group or a mentor in your recovery community who you can be honest with. Share the struggles you're facing and let them share their experiences with you. In this environment of honesty and mutual support, you can find encouragement to continue moving forward.

- Action Step: Actively participate in a group setting where you can be a light to others. Reflect on how your journey can inspire and support someone else who might be struggling with similar challenges.

- Why It Matters: Support and accountability from others are crucial for sustained growth and healing. Sharing your truth and hearing others' stories builds a sense of community and reminds you that you're not alone in your struggles.

5. Warriors of Faith: Serve Others

- Action Step: Find an opportunity to serve in your community or recovery group. Service to others is a tangible way of living out the principle of "keeping it real." Whether offering your time to help someone, sharing your testimony, or encouraging someone who is struggling, your service reflects the transformation God has worked in you.

- Action Step: Consider adopting the warrior mentality discussed in this chapter by identifying one way you can channel your passion into furthering God's kingdom. This could involve helping others or dedicating your energy to a cause that aligns with your values. If Elijah's life doesn't resonate with you, consider these other biblical characters who demonstrated incredible faith and commitment:

- Moses: Known for his leadership and unwavering faith, Moses led the Israelites out of Egypt despite overwhelming challenges. His story teaches us the power of trusting God's plan, even when it seems impossible.

- Mary (the mother of Jesus): Mary's obedience and humility in accepting God's call to bear the Savior of the world exemplifies submission to God's will. Her life reminds us of the importance of saying "yes" to God, even when it's difficult or requires great sacrifice.

- John the Baptist: John's fervent passion for preparing the way for Jesus led him to boldly proclaim the truth, no matter the cost. His life calls us to live with zeal and purpose, sharing the gospel and standing firm in our faith.

- Job: Job's perseverance in the face of immense suffering and loss showcases the importance of trusting God, even when life feels unbearable. His story teaches us that maintaining faith through trials can lead to restoration and greater understanding of God's sovereignty.

- Jesus himself: Jesus, the ultimate example of sacrificial love, service, and obedience to the Father, is the ultimate warrior of faith. His life challenges us to lay down our lives for others, serving selflessly and living with a focus on God's kingdom.

- Why It Matters: Serving others shifts the focus from yourself to the needs of others, allowing you to live out the transformation God is working in you. It strengthens your faith, encourages others, and helps you grow into the person God has called you to be. Just like these warriors of faith, you can channel your passion and purpose into making a lasting impact for God's kingdom.

These action steps guide you in "keeping it real" through honest reflection, daily discipline, patience, community support, and service. As you incorporate these practices into your life, you not only continue your journey of recovery but also embrace God's work of transformation. Trust that he is with you every step of the way and that each action brings you closer to the person he has created you to be.

6

Priorities for Living

RECOVERY IS A SHARED experience. True fellowship and support within a community are essential for ongoing healing. It's through group involvement and the encouragement of others that we find the strength to keep moving forward. By opening ourselves to our brothers and sisters, we allow God to work through their support and shared wisdom. Whether through faith-based recovery groups such as Celebrate Recovery (CR), mentors, life coaches, or Alcoholics Anonymous (AA)/Narcotics Anonymous (NA), these communities provide direction, accountability, and the essential support needed to nurture our growth. With the support of others, we draw strength from the collective wisdom of those who understand our journey. Over time, as we continue healing, we become examples to others, offering hope, strength, and a tangible reminder of the possibilities through the LORD. God's plan is always unfolding, using us to positively impact those around us. Even when we may not fully understand our influence, this is the heart of engaging with others in the community.

As we come together, it's vital to be open and honest about our struggles. A supportive community creates a safe space where we can confront our shortcomings without fear of judgment, focusing instead on healing through Christ's power. In these moments, we recognize that in our weakness, God's love becomes tangible through the support and grace of those walking alongside us. It's in this shared journey that we're reminded we don't have to carry the burden alone—God's love is made evident through the relationships within our support systems. These connections strengthen us, affirm our worth, and inspire us to keep moving forward in faith.

THE TOP-DOWN APPROACH: EMBRACING GOD'S POWER

A key principle in successful recovery is the top-down approach—seeking God first, allowing his Spirit to guide us, and turning inward for direction. It is through alignment with Christ that we find healing. Therefore, our spiritual journey must remain central as we build our new life.

Even as we experience healing, we must remain aware that the spirit of addiction or any negative force can try to creep back into our renewed hearts. In Luke 11, Jesus warns that when our lives are swept clean but we don't fill that emptiness with the Holy Spirit, we become vulnerable to negative forces once again. It's not enough to simply remove the bad; we must actively invite God's presence to dwell within us, filling every part of our lives and protecting us from the enemy's attempts to reclaim what God has redeemed. This serves as a powerful reminder that recovery is not a one-time event—it's a lifelong, ongoing process.

Sometimes, it's easy to slip into self-reliance or pride, thinking we've conquered our struggles. But we must remember that recovery isn't about controlling our addiction through human effort—it's about surrendering daily to God's incredible power. This doesn't mean we reject the effort or hard work needed for recovery; it simply means we recognize that true healing and strength come from God, not from ourselves. Embracing this truth frees us from the need to control every aspect of our lives. By living with a top-down philosophy, we allow God to handle what truly matters, and as a result, the smaller things fall into place.

The top-down approach involves inviting the LORD into our recovery process, recognizing that he alone is the source of our strength and wisdom. As we allow God to lead us, he fills us with the courage, conviction, and direction necessary to navigate any situation. In this surrender, we find peace, knowing that our healing and transformation are securely in his hands.

BEWARE OF THE CULT OF PERSONALITY

In any religious or recovery setting, it's important to be mindful of the influences we allow into our lives. While guidance and mentorship are important, we must guard against falling into the trap of the cult of personality—where human leaders are elevated above the example and importance of Christ. When we place too much emphasis on any person, no matter how gifted or charismatic, we risk losing sight of the true source of our recovery: Jesus Christ.

Jesus warns us against the dangers of seeking strength from anyone other than him. In the book of Matthew, he cautions, "But you are not to be called rabbi, for you have one teacher, and you are all brethren. And call no man your father on earth, for you have one Father, who is in heaven. Neither be called masters, for you have one master, the Christ" (Matt 23:8–10). This passage reminds us that while human leaders may guide and inspire us, they are not the ultimate source of our transformation. Christ is at the center of our recovery, and any leader or figure who shifts the focus from him to themselves is leading us away from the truth.

Therefore, we should be cautious to not idolize others, regardless of how influential or inspirational they may be. We honor the work of the Holy Spirit in their lives, but we recognize that all glory, honor, and praise belong to God alone. By keeping our focus on Christ, we remain grounded in the true source of our healing, trusting in him as our Savior, Redeemer, and Guide throughout every step of our journey.

As John writes (referring to the Holy Spirit):

I write this to you about those who would deceive you;
but the anointing which you received from him abides
in you, and you have no need that any one should teach
you; as his anointing teaches you about everything, and
is true, and is no lie, just as it has taught you, abide in
him. (1 John 2:26–27)

Our direction comes from the Holy Spirit, who dwells within
us and leads us into all truth. God's word, through the Bible and
illuminated by the Spirit, is the true guide for our lives. The Holy
Spirit opens our eyes to the deeper truths of the gospel and guides
us on the path to recovery.

FREEDOM THROUGH CHRIST

True recovery and freedom in Christ require a shift in perspective.
It's about fully embracing Christ's redemptive power—seeing life
from God's viewpoint—to heal our minds, hearts, and lives. While
the world offers countless solutions to many problems, as believers, we are called to remember that Christ has already met our
needs through his life, death, and resurrection. In him, we find the
ultimate remedy for all our concerns.

In the book of Mark, Jesus rebukes Peter for failing to understand his imminent suffering and death, emphasizing the difference between human and divine perspectives. The passage reads,
"But turning and seeing his disciples, he rebuked Peter, and said,
'Get behind me, Satan! For you are not on the side of God, but of
men'" (Mark 8:33). Peter's response to Jesus's suffering was rooted
in human logic, not divine insight. He could not see that salvation
and freedom would come through the LORD's suffering. Jesus's
strong rebuke serves as a reminder for us to align ourselves with
God's wisdom rather than relying on the shortsighted and often
misguided viewpoints of our human perspective.

In our journey, it's tempting to seek quick fixes, external sources of wisdom, or rely on our own abilities. However, the solution to
addiction and dependency is not found in the world's systems but
in surrendering to the transformative power of Christ. Jesus is the

answer—he offers complete and eternal freedom: freedom from sin, addiction, shame, and the brokenness of this world.

As we trust and rely on his grace and strength each day, we make progress in our new life, knowing that we are not dependent on the world's approach or the finite wisdom of man but on the eternal truth of God. We walk in the freedom that Christ has already secured for us through his death and resurrection. In doing so, our lives become living testimonies to the power of God's redeeming love.

DISCERNMENT AND SPIRITUAL STRENGTH

Spiritual discernment is essential in our recovery journey. As we grow in Christ, we become more attuned to his voice, allowing us to hear and follow him amid the distractions of daily life. The more we surrender to the Holy Spirit, the clearer his guidance becomes. This deeper connection empowers us to apply the wisdom the Spirit imparts to our lives, helping us navigate recovery with purpose.

We start to recognize the subtle promptings of the Spirit—like a trail of breadcrumbs guiding us through a dense forest. Through this discernment, we gain the strength to make decisions that align with God's will, remain steadfast on our path, and experience continual renewal as we stay connected to him.

As we practice discernment, we begin to recognize signs that confirm we're on the right path. God's guidance can manifest in many ways: through our interactions with others, the events we experience, the trials we face, and even the places we find ourselves. The deeper meaning behind what may seem like insignificant moments often becomes clear only after time has passed—whether days, months, or even years. During these times, patience is key. What may feel like drifting is actually part of the process of drawing closer to the LORD. Even when it doesn't seem that way, he is steadily guiding us closer to him.

This is God's perfect timing at work—and it's where our faith becomes vital. We must trust that he knows exactly what he's doing, even when we don't fully understand it ourselves. In time, we will.

In 1 Cor 2:9, Paul cites the prophet Isaiah: "But, as it is written, 'What no eye has seen, nor ear heard, nor the heart of man conceived, what God has prepared for those who love him.'" God has plans for us that far exceed our wildest imaginations, and our recovery is about stepping into the unique calling he has placed in our lives. Spiritual discernment is the key to recognizing and embracing that calling, even when the road seems unclear or uncertain. As we grow in our relationship with God and rely on the Holy Spirit, he reveals the purpose he has for us, guiding us through our challenges and into the fullness of the life he has prepared. With his wisdom, we can trust that each step we take brings us closer to the abundant life God desires for us.

LIVING WITH CONFIDENCE IN THE HOLY SPIRIT

In a world that constantly encourages us to seek answers outwardly—whether through trends, theories, philosophies, systems of understanding, or the approval of others—it's crucial to cultivate the spiritual discipline of turning inward. This isn't a call for isolation or an exploration of abstract, metaphysical concepts but a reminder to align our inner compass with the Holy Spirit as our true north. Popular culture often minimizes the role God plays in our lives, pushing us to rely on external sources for guidance. In doing so, it leads us further away from the true source of wisdom and understanding, to our detriment.

When we turn inward, we begin to realize that we are not self-sufficient. Society celebrates virtues like self-reliance, willpower, independence, and the fruits of our own labor. However, as followers of the LORD, we know that true strength and genuine independence come not from striving on our own but from surrendering to God's power. The battle for our recovery, healing, and growth isn't won through sheer will alone but through yielding to the Holy Spirit, who empowers us to walk in victory. As we are filled with his strength, the distractions, temptations, and anxieties of the world lose their hold over us.

In 2 Cor 12:9–10, Paul writes:

> But he said to me, "My grace is sufficient for you, for my power is made perfect in weakness." I will all the more gladly boast of my weaknesses, that the power of Christ may rest upon me. For the sake of Christ, then, I am content with weaknesses, insults, hardships, persecutions, and calamities; for when I am weak, then I am strong.

This is a profound truth: we are strongest when we acknowledge our weaknesses and recognize our constant need for God's grace and power. When we stop relying on the world's ways and surrender to God's will, we open ourselves to be shaped by him. It is in our vulnerability and humility that Christ's strength shines most brightly.

In the book of John, Jesus makes a powerful promise that the Father would send the Holy Spirit to be with us forever. He says:

> And I will ask the Father, and he will give you another Counselor, to be with you for ever, even the Spirit of truth, whom the world cannot receive, because it neither sees him nor knows him; you know him, for he dwells with you, and will be in you. (John 14:16–17)

The Holy Spirit is our helper and Counselor, guiding us to make wise and sound choices. He strengthens us when we are weak, offering the support we need to endure challenges. When we face pain or grief, the Spirit provides comfort and peace, reminding us of God's constant presence and love. Through the Holy Spirit, we come to understand the depths of God's love for us and learn how to reflect that love to others.

Turning inward doesn't mean retreating from the world or isolating ourselves. Instead, it means aligning our hearts with God's will and deepening our connection with him. This alignment enables us to move through our chaotic world with purpose, clarity, and focus. As we remain open to his guidance, we are empowered by his Spirit to navigate life's struggles. This inner alignment keeps us grounded in God's truth, preventing us from being swayed by the demands and distractions of the world. In practice, we become vessels of his love and strength, carrying his light into every situation.

TRUE CONFIDENCE: ROOTED IN CHRIST ALONE

When we turn inward to the Holy Spirit, our identity is profoundly transformed. Our sense of worth and confidence no longer comes from past achievements, approval from others, or the ever-changing standards of the world. Instead, it is firmly anchored in the unshakable truth that we are beloved children of God, fully redeemed and empowered through the blood of Christ. This shift in identity frees us from seeking validation in external sources, allowing us to walk confidently in the security of God's love and grace.

Paul reminds us, "I can do all things in him who strengthens me" (Phil 4:13). This confidence doesn't come from our own abilities or willpower but from knowing Christ personally and experientially. It's about recognizing his power at work within us, especially in our weakest moments. When we trust in the LORD, he equips us to move forward in our recovery, even in the face of setbacks or struggles. It's this deep, unwavering trust in his strength that propels us through challenges, knowing that, with him, nothing is impossible.

THE DANGERS OF LOOKING TO THE WORLD FOR FULFILLMENT

The world is full of promises that claim to bring fulfillment, yet time and time again, they prove empty. Society offers fulfillment through personal satisfaction and worldly success, but in the end, these promises reveal themselves as useless. Earthly pursuits cannot satisfy the deep spiritual hunger within us.

In contrast, turning inward toward Christ's presence and the guidance of the Holy Spirit gives us a peace and joy that surpasses anything the world can offer. Jesus assures us, "Peace I leave with you; my peace I give to you; not as the world gives do I give to you. Let not your hearts be troubled, neither let them be afraid" (John 14:27). The peace Christ offers is not based on our circumstances—it rises above the turmoil, struggles, and uncertainties of life. It fills the emptiness that the world cannot touch, bringing a deep sense of calm and security that only God can provide.

In recovery, it's essential to recognize that our fulfillment is not dependent on external circumstances or the ever-changing tides of life—it is anchored in Christ, who is unchanging, eternally faithful, and always present. While the world may define success and happiness based on material achievements, social approval, or consumption, we are called to shift our focus away from society's transient values and center our hearts on the LORD. By doing so, we reject the pull of worldliness and embrace the lasting peace and purpose that only Christ can provide.

THE DAILY CHOICE: SEEKING GOD'S GUIDANCE OVER WORLDLY SOLUTIONS

Each day, we are faced with a choice: to look inward to God for guidance or to seek solutions from the world. When we look outward, we often feel frustrated, anxious, or overwhelmed. However, when we turn inward and seek God's presence within us, we discover the peace and clarity that only a personal relationship with him can provide.

This is not a one-time decision; it is a continual practice of surrendering to God's will. Our commitment to sobriety is deeply connected to our ongoing choice to seek the Holy Spirit's guidance through prayer, reflection, and engagement with Scripture. Turning inward doesn't mean retreating from the world or withdrawing from life—it means choosing to rely on God's strength and trusting his Spirit to lead us, regardless of the circumstances.

We should continually remind ourselves that our true source of power and strength is God, not the world or anything it offers. As we place our trust in him, we experience a confidence that transcends life's temporary struggles. This confidence is grounded in the unshakable foundation of our identity in Christ, providing an ongoing source of strength and resilience as we navigate our recovery and explore our unique gifts from God.

As we continue on our journey, we begin to discover the individual talents God has entrusted to each of us. These blessings are not only for our personal growth but also for the good of those around us. When we embrace and use these gifts, we become part of something much bigger—contributing to the healing and restoration of others while deepening our own connection to God's purpose for our lives.

REFLECTION QUESTIONS

1. The Role of Community and Trust in God's Plan: If you have a recovery community, how has it supported you on your journey, offering strength and encouragement when you needed it most? Are there people in your life whom you can trust to walk alongside you in this journey? If you do not have a community, where will you begin to find one?

2. Validation from External Sources: In what areas of your recovery have you sought answers or validation from external sources? How can you turn inward to Christ and rely on his Holy Spirit for the strength, wisdom, and guidance you need today?

3. Discerning True Guidance and Avoiding False Influences: How can you more effectively discern the voice of the Holy Spirit amidst external pressures, ensuring that Christ remains your ultimate source of strength and recovery?

4. Taking Personal Responsibility and Embracing Freedom: How can you embrace the responsibility of your own recovery while fully trusting in Christ's guidance? How can you protect your heart from the distractions of the cult of personality and other influences that seek to pull you away from his path?

FAITH IN ACTION: PRIORITIES FOR LIVING

Recovery is a continuous journey of growth and deeper connection with God and others. The truths discussed in this chapter serve as a foundation for building a strong, lasting recovery—one rooted in faith, community, and God's guidance. Below are ways you can apply the key insights from this chapter to your own life:

1. Engage in a Supportive Community

   - Action Step: Seek out a group or community that aligns with your values and recovery goals, such as Celebrate Recovery (or another faith-based recovery group), Alcoholics Anonymous, or Narcotics Anonymous. Commit to attending regularly, and be open and honest about your struggles. Vulnerability is key to healing. Sharing your journey with others not only builds accountability but also fosters a deeper sense of connection and support. The strength of these communities lies in mutual openness, where every individual's courage to be vulnerable can inspire and uplift others.

   - Why It Matters: Being part of a community provides encouragement, accountability, and a shared sense of purpose in your recovery. Engaging with others who understand your struggles creates a safe space for growth. Vulnerability with others allows you to receive support, and through that shared journey, you can experience healing together, knowing you are not alone.

2. Surrender to God Daily

   - Action Step: Begin each day with a prayer of surrender, asking God to lead your steps and fill you with his strength. Remember that recovery is an ongoing process—don't rely on your own strength, but lean on God's power.

   - Personal Reflection: I have a designated spot in my bedroom for prayer. Each day, after I make my bed and before I go to sleep, I spend time there for prayer, reflection, and sometimes even crying as I connect with the Almighty. I've learned that when I don't make God a priority, I tend to make poor decisions and drift away from the course he has for me. That quiet time with him is essential for keeping my life grounded.

- Why It Matters: The top-down approach means inviting God to guide your recovery. When you surrender daily, you allow his Spirit to lead and transform you instead of relying on your own limited strength. Surrendering daily enables you to tap into his limitless power, not your own, providing everlasting healing and growth.

3. Keep Christ at the Center

- Action Step: Reflect on Matt 23:8–10 and avoid putting anyone on a pedestal in your recovery process. While mentors and leaders are helpful, always direct your focus back to Christ, the true source of your healing.

- Why It Matters: While people can inspire and guide you, no one can replace Christ as the center of your recovery. Keeping your eyes on Jesus protects you from being misled by human figures and ensures you're walking in truth. When Christ is at the center, he guides your recovery and empowers you to walk in freedom.

4. Pursue Freedom Through Christ's Perspective

- Action Step: Shift your perspective to align with God's view of freedom, not the world's. Instead of looking to external solutions, surrender your desires to Christ, and allow his redemptive power to heal you.

- Why It Matters: True freedom comes from embracing Christ's power over your life. The world's solutions are temporary, but in Christ, we find eternal healing, peace, and purpose that transcend earthly satisfaction. This perspective allows you to let go of worldly dependencies and step into a life of lasting freedom in Christ.

5. Develop Spiritual Discernment

   • Action Step: Continue to spend time each day in quiet reflection and prayer, seeking God's guidance. Pay attention to the small, seemingly insignificant moments where his Spirit is leading you. Ask him to sharpen your ability to discern his voice.

   • Why It Matters: The more you practice discernment, the clearer God's guidance becomes. This wisdom helps you make decisions that align with his will and keep you on the path to healing. Discernment leads you to the right choices, ensuring that you remain faithful and steadfast on your journey.

6. Avoid the Temptation to Look to the World for Fulfillment

   • Action Step: Challenge yourself to examine where you are looking for fulfillment outside of Christ. When you face moments of temptation or dissatisfaction, turn to God and his promises, rather than seeking worldly satisfaction.

   • Why It Matters: The world offers temporary fulfillment that leaves us empty. True peace comes from Christ alone. By focusing on him, you will experience a deep sense of contentment and joy that surpasses anything the world offers. Turning inward to Christ ensures that you're grounded in eternal peace, not the fleeting distractions of the world.

7. Make the Daily Choice to Seek God's Guidance

   • Action Step: Each morning, choose to seek God's guidance over worldly solutions. Prioritize time in Scripture, prayer, and reflection to center your heart on God's will. Trust that, no matter what the day brings, he is in control and will guide you.

   • Why It Matters: Each day is a new opportunity to surrender to God's will. When you choose to rely on his guidance instead of the world's solutions, you invite peace and clarity into your life and recovery. Seeking God's guidance each day strengthens your foundation in Christ, making it easier to navigate life's challenges with his wisdom and grace.

8. Be Mindful of Crutches

- Action Step: Stay vigilant for any behaviors or habits that may replace your previous addiction. These may include social media, gaming, pornography, caffeine, sex, energy drinks, tobacco, or even thrill-seeking activities. Identify which of these are consuming your time and focus, and evaluate whether they are distracting you from growing closer to God. Seek God's help in discerning which of these behaviors are taking root in your life and begin to set boundaries or take intentional breaks to focus on spiritual growth.

- Why it Matters: Lesser addictions or crutches can subtly replace the emptiness once filled by addiction, shifting your reliance from God to these behaviors. They can distract you from your true source of strength and healing. By remaining vigilant, you protect your relationship with God, ensuring that your devotion is undivided. When you surrender these crutches, you open yourself to deeper intimacy with God, allowing him to be the true fulfillment and refuge you need.

By applying these steps, you actively engage in your recovery journey, keeping Christ at the center and seeking his guidance every day. Each step you take in faith brings you closer to the person God has created you to be, equipped to live a life of purpose through him.

7

Gifts from the Holy Spirit

IN 1 COR 12:7, Paul teaches us, "To each is given the manifestation of the Spirit for the common good." This is a profound truth. The gifts we receive from the Holy Spirit are not meant for personal gain or advancement; they are intended to be shared with others for the building up of the body of Christ. Each of us has been given a unique combination of spiritual gifts which we are called to discover, cultivate, and use to serve and bless others. These gifts are tools through which God works, bringing healing, wisdom, and restoration to a broken world. As children of God, we are created to be instruments of his peace, each in our own special way.

Later in the same chapter, we are introduced to a wide range of spiritual gifts that the Holy Spirit may manifest in our lives:

> To one is given through the Spirit the utterance of wisdom, and to another the utterance of knowledge according to the same Spirit, to another faith by the same Spirit, to another gifts of healing by the one Spirit, to another the working of miracles, to another prophecy, to another the ability to distinguish between spirits, to another various kinds of tongues, to another the interpretation of tongues. (1 Cor 12:8–10)

Though these gifts may vary, they share one common purpose: to strengthen the church and glorify God. No gift is greater or lesser than another; each one is essential to the work of God's kingdom. While we don't choose the gifts the Holy Spirit bestows upon us, we should remain open and receptive to the blessings God has entrusted to us. Each gift is uniquely designed to the role he has prepared for us.

OPERATING IN GOD'S TIMING, NOT OURS

One of the most challenging aspects of receiving and using spiritual gifts is recognizing that God works according to his perfect timing. In Acts 1:7, as Jesus speaks of his ascension, he tells his disciples, "It is not for you to know times or seasons which the Father has fixed by his own authority." In today's culture driven by instant gratification, we often struggle with impatience. Yet, throughout Scripture, Jesus reminds us that it is not our role to determine when or how God's plan will unfold. Instead, we are called to trust in our heavenly Father's perfect timing and remain faithful as we walk in our journey.

Remaining faithful can be especially challenging, as it often requires a shift in our mindset. Instead of focusing on personal desires, accomplishments, or timelines, contentment comes when we align ourselves with God's purpose. When we shift from trying to control outcomes to trusting in God's perfect timing, we open ourselves to becoming vessels of his peace and love, living in harmony with the rhythms of his plan for our lives.

LIVING WITH PURPOSE, NOT
PURSUING FULFILLMENT

We live in a world that relentlessly urges us to pursue individual happiness, material success, and personal achievement. However, God's way stands in stark contrast to this mindset. Our purpose in life isn't to seek fulfillment on our own terms but to allow God's fulfillment to flow through us as we align with his plan. True joy and peace don't come from achieving our desires because our understanding of what truly brings happiness is limited—something we've learned through our struggles with substance abuse. Instead, true happiness is found in embracing the life that God has lovingly designed for us. When we stop chasing after our own fleeting ideas of happiness and instead focus on fulfilling God's will, we open ourselves to a deeper, more meaningful life through the practice of our gifts.

ALIGNING WITH GOD'S PURPOSE IN RECOVERY

When we embrace the gifts that God has designed specifically for us, our lives take on greater purpose. We are called to serve in distinct ways—whether by offering wisdom, sharing knowledge, providing emotional support, or walking alongside others on their journey. While recovery begins as a personal healing process, we quickly discover that lasting healing is found in serving others. Just as we have received grace, we are called to extend that grace to those around us. Joining a Christian faith community is a natural way to explore and sharpen our gifts. In doing so, we experience the profound satisfaction of knowing our lives have meaning and purpose that goes beyond our own recovery.

As we embrace this truth, we are called to fully trust in God's plan and timing. We don't need to know every detail of how or when God will use us; we simply need to remain open to receiving and using the gifts he has given us. This requires surrender—trusting that God knows what's best for us, even when our circumstances don't make sense at the time. He will equip us with everything we need, and in his perfect timing, he will use us to accomplish his purposes in the world. When we remember that our lives are not about us but about God working through us, we align ourselves with his plan and boldly step into the abundant life he's promised with our newly discovered talents.

To fully live out God's plan, we must also reject the influences of the world that seek to distract and corrupt the work he is doing in us. Just as we have been given new gifts, we must guard ourselves against worldly desires and temptation. These things can slowly permeate and undermine the transformation God is bringing about in us. By rejecting the things that keep us from fully living in his will, we remain focused on what truly matters—his purpose for our lives and his eternal plan.

REFLECTION QUESTIONS

1. Recognizing Your Gifts: How do you recognize and embrace the spiritual gifts God has entrusted to you? In what ways have you witnessed these gifts at work in your own recovery and in supporting others? How can you actively seek to discern the unique gifts God has placed within you and use them for his glory and the betterment of those around you?

2. Resisting God's Timing: In what areas of your life do you find yourself struggling with impatience or resisting God's timing? How can you learn to trust in his perfect plan, surrender control, and embrace the process, knowing that his timing is always right?

3. Shifting Your Focus: How does shifting your focus from seeking personal happiness to embracing God's purpose transform your daily life and recovery journey? What specific steps can you take today to align more closely with God's plan for you and to prioritize serving others over personal gain?

FAITH IN ACTION: GIFTS FROM THE HOLY SPIRIT

God has uniquely gifted each of us with talents and abilities that reflect his love, creativity, and purpose for our lives. These gifts are not just for our personal enjoyment or success but are meant to be used to serve others and glorify him. In this chapter, we've explored how gifts from God are an integral part of our lives and recovery, and now it's time to take action to discover, develop, and use those gifts to their fullest potential. Below are some practical steps to help you identify and live out the gifts God has given you:

1. Spend Time in Prayer and Reflection

   - Action Step: Take time each day to pray and ask God to reveal the gifts he has placed in your life. Ask the Holy Spirit to guide you in recognizing your strengths and abilities. Reflect on the times when you've felt joy, peace, or fulfillment (without substances)—these moments often align with the gifts God has given you.

   - Why It Matters: Prayer and reflection create space for God to speak to your heart. When you actively seek his guidance, you open yourself up to his revelation and deeper understanding of your unique gifts. The Holy Spirit will give you insight into your potential and how to use it for his purposes.

2. Take an Inventory of Your Strengths

   - Action Step: Make a list of your natural abilities, talents, and interests. Think about what you are good at—whether it's listening, teaching, organizing, leading, or creating something with your hands. Consider times when others have complimented or asked for your help. These are clues to your gifts.

   - Why It Matters: Understanding your strengths helps you see how you can contribute to others in meaningful ways. God has intentionally placed these abilities within you, and they are not by accident! Identifying them helps you recognize where you can serve and how you can grow in your purpose.

3. Explore Opportunities to Serve

   - Action Step: Find opportunities to serve in your church, community, or recovery group. Whether it's volunteering at a local shelter, leading a small group, cooking or serving food at a soup kitchen, or helping with administrative tasks, serving others allows you to put your gifts into action. Reflect on how you can use your unique talents to meet the needs of others and contribute to the greater good.

- Why It Matters: Serving others is one of the most effective ways to discover how your gifts can be used for God's glory. When you step out in faith and take action, you not only help others, but you also gain clarity on the specific ways God has equipped you to serve. Serving builds confidence in your abilities, strengthens your faith, and draws you closer to God's will for your life. Remember Jesus. He came to serve, not to be served, and through his service, he demonstrated true greatness. By serving, you follow in his footsteps, becoming more like him in both humility and purpose.

4. Seek Mentorship and Guidance

- Action Step: Find someone who can mentor you or offer spiritual guidance in your journey of discovering your gifts. This could be a priest or pastor, a person of faith, or a leader in your church or recovery group. Ask them to help you identify your strengths and areas where you can grow.

- Personal Reflection: I've had the privilege of working with an old sage nun over the years for spiritual direction. When I began my journey with Sister Nancy, I thought she would give me direct answers to my most pressing questions. I became frustrated when, instead of offering the guidance I expected, she repeatedly advised me to look within and find the answers by listening to the Holy Spirit. After a few months of attending our regular sessions, I even considered quitting because I wasn't getting the answers I thought I needed when I wanted them. I'm so glad I stuck with it because I learned a very valuable lesson—one that, in large part, is the point of this entire book!

- Why It Matters: A mentor can provide valuable insight and encouragement as you navigate discovering and using your

gifts. They can help you see your strengths from a different perspective and offer wisdom on how to develop them
further for God's kingdom. A mentor helps you realize that
sometimes, the answers we seek aren't always what we expect but are often found in patience and self-reflection.

5. Step Out of Your Comfort Zone

- Action Step: Take a step of faith by trying something
new that aligns with your gifts. If you're passionate about
teaching, offer to lead a Bible study or teach a class. If
you're an encourager, start reaching out to others in your
recovery group to offer support and guidance.

- Why It Matters: Growth happens when we step outside of
our comfort zone. It may feel intimidating at first, but taking that step is essential to realizing your potential. God
doesn't just call us to discover our gifts; he calls us to use
them. Stepping out in faith gives God the opportunity to
work through you and refine your gifts.

6. Allow God to Develop Your Gifts

- Action Step: Commit to ongoing personal growth. Read
books, attend workshops, and seek training opportunities that will help you develop your gifts. Engage in daily
Scripture reading and prayer to grow in your relationship
with God, as spiritual growth will deepen your understanding of how to use your gifts effectively.

- Why It Matters: Gifts are meant to be developed, not just
discovered. Just as a muscle grows stronger with exercise,
your gifts will grow as you nurture and develop them.
God has given you these gifts, but he wants you to steward
them well. As you grow spiritually and personally, your
ability to use your gifts will become more refined and
powerful for his glory.

7. Trust God with the Impact of Your Gifts

- Action Step: When you use your gifts, trust that God will work through them, regardless of the immediate results. You may not always see the impact right away, but trust that your faithfulness to use your gifts will make a difference in ways you cannot always see.

- Why It Matters: We often want to see immediate results, but God works in his own timing. Trusting him with the impact of your gifts reminds you that your purpose is not about your own success but about serving his greater plan. When you trust God with the outcome, you release the pressure and allow him to use your gifts in ways that align with his perfect will.

8. Celebrate the Diversity of Gifts in the Body of Christ

- Action Step: Take time to appreciate the gifts of others in your recovery group, church, or community. Celebrate the ways in which others are using their gifts to serve and encourage you. Acknowledge the ways God has uniquely gifted everyone, and support others in using their gifts.

- Why It Matters: Recognizing the diversity of gifts helps you see the bigger picture of how God is working in his body. No one gift is more important than another. By celebrating the gifts of others, you affirm that God has a unique role for each person, and you encourage a spirit of unity and collaboration.

By taking these action steps, you actively engage in discovering, developing, and using the unique gifts God has entrusted to you. These gifts are not only integral to your recovery journey, but they also serve a greater purpose—bringing glory to God and blessing others. As you step out in faith and put your talents into action, you'll witness the transformative power of aligning your gifts with God's plan for your life. In serving others and living out your purpose, you'll draw closer to his will and experience the fullness of the life he has called you to live.

8

Reject the Worldly Leaven

As we step into the abundant life that God offers through the Holy Spirit, it is essential to remain vigilant against the powerful forces that try to pull us back into old patterns of thinking and living. We should consciously reject the mindset and belief system of this world that keeps us trapped in a cycle of scarcity, constantly pushing us to seek more. Society bombards us with messages that define our worth by external factors—wealth, status, possessions, success, and power. However, God's kingdom operates on a completely different economy. In his kingdom, our identity and purpose are not found in what we accumulate or achieve, nor in our past, but in who we are in Christ.

As active addicts, we spent much of our time chasing external fixes—substances, possessions, or approval from others—believing they could fill the emptiness inside. We were conditioned, or conditioned ourselves, to think that fulfillment and happiness were found in the next high, the next material possession, or the next achievement. But through God's grace, we are invited into a life that overflows with his love, peace, joy, and purpose—gifts that flow freely from a deep, abiding relationship with the Holy Spirit, not from external circumstances.

The process of recovery is as much about transforming the mind as it is about healing the body and soul. Paul writes in Romans, "Do not be conformed to this world but be transformed by the renewal of your mind, that you may prove what is the will of God, what is good and acceptable and perfect" (Rom 12:2). The renewal of our minds is critical to walking in the abundant life that Christ offers us. It begins with rejecting the false narratives of scarcity that the world wants us to believe and by embracing the truth of God's abundant provision.

UNDERSTANDING THE LEAVEN OF
THE PHARISEES AND HEROD

Jesus cautioned his disciples, "Take heed, beware of the leaven of the Pharisees and the leaven of Herod" (Mark 8:15). In this warning, the term "leaven" is symbolic of the subtle, yet powerful ideas and worldviews that can creep into our hearts and minds, infecting our entire way of thinking. Just as leaven works its way through dough, eventually affecting the whole loaf, worldly mindsets can infiltrate our hearts, shaping the way we view ourselves, God, and others.

Jesus specifically warns against the leaven of two groups: the Pharisees and Herod. The Pharisees represent self-righteousness—the belief that we can earn God's favor by following rules and rituals. They embodied the mindset that salvation and favor must be earned through external actions or that a relationship with God was secondary. The Pharisees' legalistic view was rooted in the belief that we must prove our worth through performance, rather than receiving grace freely.

Herod, on the other hand, represents the worldview driven by power, materialism, and the belief that happiness is found through wealth, political power, and control. This mindset often leads people to equate success with accumulation, resulting in a fruitless pursuit of happiness. Herod's way of thinking operates on the belief that the world's systems will provide what we need. Both mindsets—the Pharisees' self-righteousness and Herod's material-ism—stem from the idea of scarcity. This philosophy perpetuates the idea that there is never enough—whether it is time, money, love, or resources.

Jesus challenges the scarcity mindset, offering us a new way to live—one rooted in the abundance of God's provision. In the miracle where Jesus feeds four thousand hungry people (Mark 8), he demonstrates that in God's economy, there is always more than enough. Even with only seven loaves of bread and a few small fish, Jesus multiplied the food, feeding thousands, with seven baskets of leftovers remaining. This miracle reveals the truth that in Christ, there is more than enough—more than enough grace, more than enough love, and more than enough provision. We do not have to live in fear of running out, because God is abundant in his provision for us.

REJECTING THE WORLD'S SCARCITY MINDSET

Rejecting the worldly mindset means rejecting the lie of scarcity. The systems of this world want us to believe we are defined by what we lack. They tell us we are incomplete, insufficient, and un-worthy unless we acquire certain things or achieve specific goals. Our hyper-secularized society bombards us daily with messages of need, insisting that we must have more—more money, more power, more possessions, more success—to be happy. But this mindset only leads to emptiness. No matter how much we gain in the material world, it is never enough. The addiction epidemic it-self stands as proof. We can chase after all the substances the world offers, seeking happiness, but in the end, they can never satisfy the deepest longings of our soul.

As recovering addicts, we've learned the painful truth that substances or worldly possessions cannot fulfill our deepest needs. We chased after the next high or fix, thinking these things could fill the emptiness inside us. But instead, they left us more broken and lost. Now, through God's grace, we understand the truth: true happiness, fulfillment, and peace do not come from external circumstances but from a restored relationship with God.

Rejecting the world's scarcity mindset requires a shift in how we view ourselves and our place in the world. Rather than believing we are insufficient or incomplete, we can embrace the truth that, in Christ, we are more than enough. In him, we have everything we need for life—period.

This doesn't mean we won't face challenges or hardships. However, it means that even in times of difficulty, we can find peace and contentment, living in the light, knowing we are defined not by what we lack but by Christ's sufficiency.

THE LEAVEN OF SCARCITY IN RELIGION

Even within the Christian community, the mindset of scarcity can sometimes creep in, but in a different form. Some believers may start to rely on rules, rituals, and religious practices as a means of trying to earn favor with God. They focus on external behaviors—attending church, following certain rituals, or adhering to specific moral codes—rather than prioritizing a personal relationship with Christ.

While religious practices can certainly help us grow in our faith and strengthen our connection to God, they are not meant to replace the core of our relationship with Jesus; rather, they are an expression of our faith. The temptation may be to reduce our walk with God to a set of rules and rituals, thinking that by performing these actions, we will earn God's approval or favor. This approach is rooted in scarcity—believing that God's love and grace must be earned rather than freely received as a gift. Religious practices and community gatherings are powerful means of strengthening our connection with God. However, their true value lies not in merely going through the motions but in their ability to draw us nearer to him. When our practices and involvement in the community are motivated by love and devotion to Christ, they have the power to transform our hearts.

The gospel reveals that God's love and grace are free gifts, given to us in abundance. As Paul writes in 1 Cor 13:13, "So faith, hope, love abide, these three; but the greatest of these is love." True transformation occurs when we receive God's love and allow it to overflow into our lives. This is the heart of the Christian faith: a personal relationship with a loving, gracious God, not a checklist of rules to follow. When our hearts are rooted in his love, our actions naturally flow from that relationship—not out of obligation or a desire to earn his favor.

LIVING IN FREEDOM: REJECTING THE LEAVEN OF THE WORLD

Once we recognize the world's scarcity mindset, we can choose to disengage from it. We can reject the belief that we are incomplete or insufficient unless we have more. In Christ, we are made whole—no longer defined by what we lack but by who we are in him.

This shift in mindset is essential for our healing and recovery. It is only when we reject the world's false promises of fulfillment and embrace the abundant life offered by Christ that we can experience real freedom. This freedom is not the absence of challenges or pain but the assurance that, no matter what comes our way, God's provision is always more than enough.

In addressing mankind's daily anxieties about food, drink, and clothing, Jesus reminds us in Matt 6:33, "But seek first his kingdom and his righteousness, and all these things shall be yours as well." When we prioritize God's kingdom by placing him at the center of our lives, everything else falls into place. The LORD promises to provide for our needs, just as he abundantly provided for the four thousand hungry people. We don't need to strive for more or worry about how our daily needs will be met; we simply need to trust in God's provision and walk in the abundant life he offers.

CONFORM TO GOD'S WAY—NOT THE WORLD'S

To further cite and reiterate Paul's discussion in Romans:

> I appeal to you therefore, brethren, by the mercies of God, to present your bodies as a living sacrifice, holy and acceptable to God, which is your spiritual worship. Do not be conformed to this world but be transformed by the renewal of your mind, that you may prove what is the will of God, what is good and acceptable and perfect. (Rom 12:1-2)

Let us pray daily that the LORD helps us recognize the constant influence of media programming in our movies, TV shows, music, and advertisements. We should be aware of both the subtle and direct promotion of behaviors deemed acceptable by society yet in conflict with God's ways. These influences are part of a broader mindset that encourages scarcity and self-interest over God's abundance.

As we continue to reject the leaven of the world, let us embrace the power of God's grace and walk in the freedom that comes from knowing we are complete in Christ—his provision is always more than enough. Allowing the leaven of the world into our lives leads to despair, but when empowered by God's will, joy and everlasting life are sure to follow. Rejecting the world's lies opens us to fully appreciate every aspect of our beautiful new life in the LORD.

In this newfound liberation, we begin to see the beauty of God's work in every moment. Gratitude becomes a natural response as we recognize the blessings he has placed in our daily experience. When we live in a state of thankfulness, our perspective shifts, and we begin to notice the divine in the ordinary, finding joy in the simplest blessings. It is through gratitude that we cultivate a deeper connection with God and truly begin to live fully in the abundance of his love.

REFLECTION QUESTIONS

1. Recognizing Scarcity vs. Embracing Abundance: Where do you notice the influence of a scarcity mindset in your life—whether in your thoughts, actions, or desires? How can you intentionally shift your mindset to fully embrace God's abundance and trust in his provision? Reflect on specific steps you can take today to align with the truth that, in Christ, you already have everything you need.

2. Distinguishing a Relationship with Christ from Rituals: How can you identify when you are leaning on religious rituals or worldly systems rather than cultivating a true, personal relationship with Christ? What steps can you take to ensure your focus remains on deepening your connection with him, rather than relying on external practices or worldly solutions?

3. Living Out Freedom Responsibly in Recovery: As you experience the freedom that comes through Jesus, what specific actions can you take to live responsibly, make wise decisions, and actively support others on their journey of faith?

FAITH IN ACTION: REJECT THE WORLDLY LEAVEN

As you move forward in your journey of recovery and healing, it's crucial to put into practice the lessons of rejecting worldly mindsets and embracing the truth of God's abundant provision. The transformation of your mind is essential in living out the freedom Christ has won for you, and it starts by actively rejecting the scarcity mentality that the world promotes. Below are actionable steps to help you put this into practice in your daily life:

1. Examine Your Thought Patterns
   • Action Step: Take some time each day to reflect on your thoughts. Are you focused on what you lack or feeling stressed about external circumstances and what others think of you? Are you adopting a negative or limited

outlook on life? Write down your thoughts and evaluate whether they align with the world's mindset of scarcity or God's perspective of abundance.

- Why It Matters: Awareness is the first step to change. Recognizing when you are thinking according to the world's standards of scarcity helps you to correct your course and begin to align your thoughts with God's truth. By taking stock of your inner dialogue, you can start replacing scarcity-driven thoughts with abundant, faith-filled ones.

2. Reject External Pressures

- Action Step: Identify areas where you may be chasing after external validation, possessions, or status. Ask yourself: is this pursuit aligned with God's purpose for my life? Let go of the need to conform to the world's standards of success and take a break from anything that causes you to feel pressured by societal expectations.

- Why It Matters: By distancing yourself from the world's pressures, you create space to hear God's voice more clearly. When you let go of external expectations, you are free to embrace the identity Christ has given you, which is not based on what you have or what you achieve but on who you are in him.

3. Refocus on God's Abundant Provision

- Action Step: Begin each day by thanking God for what he has already provided—whether it's your health, relationships, recovery, or even the basics like food, shelter, and peace of mind. Reaffirm your belief that in Christ, you have more than enough. Reflect on simple blessings: Did you rest well last night? When you opened your eyes, could you see? Can you taste and smell today? Are you able to hear? Start small with gratitude and build from there!

- Why It Matters: Gratitude shifts your focus from what you don't have to what you already possess in Christ. This simple act of thanksgiving helps cultivate a heart of contentment, reminding you that God's provision is more than sufficient. It reinforces your trust in God's goodness, even during difficult times.

4. Engage in Mindful Consumption of Media

- Action Step: Be intentional about the media you consume. Watch, listen to, and read things that align with God's abundance and truth, rather than those that perpetuate scarcity or unhealthy desires. Take note of how movies, music, or advertisements make you feel. Do they encourage you to pursue things outside of God's will, or do they remind you of the abundance of God's love and grace?

- Why It Matters: The media you consume can shape your worldview, often subtly reinforcing society's mindset of scarcity. By being more mindful about what you allow into your heart and mind, you can protect yourself from influences that pull you back into old ways of thinking and behaving.

5. Prioritize Relationship Over Rituals

- Action Step: Examine your spiritual practices. Are they rituals you perform to earn God's approval, or are they expressions of your love for him? Cultivate a relationship with God by spending time with him in prayer, worship, and Scripture reading—not to check off a list of duties but to deepen your connection with the LORD, who has already given you everything you need.

- Why It Matters: The heart of our faith is not about external actions but about a relationship with God. When you focus on knowing him more deeply and personally, you move away from a mindset of scarcity (where you feel like you need to perform to earn God's love) and embrace the abundant grace he freely offers.

6. Live Out Generosity

- Action Step: Practice generosity by giving—whether it's your time, talents, or resources. Rather than hoarding or fearing you don't have enough, choose to share what you have with others. Look for opportunities to serve in your community, church, or recovery group. Trust that as you give, God will continue to provide for your needs. Consider tithing regularly as an act of faith, even if your resources are limited.

- Why It Matters: Generosity is a powerful way to reject the world's scarcity mindset. When you give freely, you declare that you trust in God's abundance and not in the limitations of the world. Serving others also helps you see that God is at work even in the small acts of kindness and reinforces the truth that you are part of his greater plan.

7. Affirm Your Identity in Christ

- Action Step: Each day, remind yourself of who you are in Christ. Your identity is not defined by what you have, what you've achieved, or what you lack. You are a beloved child of God, made complete in him. Write down affirmations based on Scripture, such as "I am chosen," "I am enough in Christ," or "God provides for all my needs." Alternatively, create a personal mantra like "I pray like a soldier" and speak these truths aloud each day.

- Why It Matters: Embracing your true identity in Christ helps you reject the lies of scarcity. When you remember who you are in God's eyes, you stop measuring your worth by worldly standards and begin to live with confidence in his provision.

8. Embrace Abundant Peace

- Action Step: When stress or anxiety about your future or needs arises, pause and center yourself in God's peace. Practice deep breathing, meditative prayer, or journaling to shift your focus from fear and lack to trust in God's provision.

- Personal Reflection: Would it surprise you to learn that this book has its origins in the daily journaling I began during the bleakness of the COVID-19 pandemic? At the time, I used journaling as a way to relieve my concerns and find clarity. I can assure you, I never set out to write a book—never even imagined that I would be here doing this. I still have my original notes, and I revisit them from time to time. It's both exciting and edifying to witness the personal growth and development that's unfolded over the years.

- Why It Matters: Peace is a sign that we are embracing God's abundance. The world offers temporary fixes, but true peace comes from knowing that, no matter the circumstances, we are safe in God's care. Living in this peace is a practical way to reject the world's mindset and walk in the freedom Christ offers. Don't give up on the routines that keep you grounded.

By taking these practical steps, you will begin to reject the false leaven of scarcity and embrace the abundant life that Christ has for you. This transformation doesn't happen overnight, but with God's help, you can renew your mind and live in the freedom of his provision. As you let go of the world's lies, you make room for God's grace to flow abundantly in your life, leading you to greater joy, contentment, and purpose.

9

Practicing Gratitude
Finding Beauty in the Everyday

As the Israelites prepared to enter the promised land, they paused for reflection during the revival at Shechem, as described in Josh 24. This moment of reflection allowed them to look back on their forty-year journey through the desert—one that, though filled with hardships, was ultimately shaped by God's liberating hand. With gratitude, they praised him for his guidance and grace, recognizing that their deliverance from Egyptian bondage and their survival in the wilderness were only possible through his divine intervention. In this sacred moment, they also reaffirmed their devotion to God, renewing their commitment to follow him faithfully.

Like the Israelites, we are called to pause and give thanks for our release from bondage and the new life we've found in our promised land—a time of personal revival. In this moment, we cultivate a heart of gratitude, reflecting on where the Lord has brought us, where we are now, and where he is leading us. With an attitude of thankfulness, we begin to notice something both simple and profound: the small, everyday gifts that God has graciously placed in our lives—on top of the gift of sobriety. These gifts, once overlooked, now become some of the most meaningful moments we can embrace on our healing journey.

Unfortunately, in the depths of addiction, we often miss these acts of kindness, numb from the desire to escape or consumed by the chaos of substance abuse. Yet, in recovery, we are called to fully embrace life and recognize the blessings the Lord has in store for us.

THE BEAUTY IN EVERYDAY MOMENTS

As we emerge from the fog of dependency, we begin to see the world around us in a new light. What once seemed insignificant now serves as a reminder of God's goodness. The radiant sunrise, marking the start of a new day, is no longer something we rush past but a moment to pause and appreciate. The golden hues of morning light become a gift from our Creator—a symbol of new beginnings. The chirping of birds, the rustling of leaves in the wind, and the simple symphony of nature's sounds invite us into a peaceful connection with the world around us—one we may have once overlooked in our pursuit of worldly pleasures.

As we journey through healing, our senses awaken to the simple pleasures of life. The aroma of a fresh cup of coffee or the satisfying flavors of a nourishing meal remind us of God's bounty and provision. It's the joy of being fully present in each moment, appreciating and cherishing life in ways we couldn't when we were trapped in our former ways. These everyday experiences are expressions of God's love and care, drawing us closer to him.

WELCOMING GRATITUDE IN OUR LIFE

Gratitude is one of the most powerful tools in recovery. When we shift our focus from what we feel we lack or struggle with to what God has already provided, we open our hearts more fully to his blessings. The simple act of being thankful—of recognizing the beauty and abundance around us—can transform our perspective on life. It reminds us that God's calming presence is found in every moment, every detail, and in the gifts he bestows upon us. As Paul says in Phil 4:6–7, "Have no anxiety about anything, but in everything by prayer and supplication with thanksgiving let your requests be made known to God. And the peace of God, which passes all understanding, will keep your hearts and your minds in Christ Jesus."

As we practice gratitude, we draw closer to God, recognizing his active role in our healing. He answers our prayers as we bring our requests before him. Gratitude shifts our focus from the pain and suffering of addiction to the beauty and grace that abound in our lives, even in the midst of struggle. Each moment of thanksgiving is an invitation to experience the peace and joy God desires for us, helping us keep our hearts and minds anchored in him.

Recovery is about encountering something far greater than ourselves. As we heal, life becomes richer, deeper, and more fulfilling. What once felt mundane now shines as an extraordinary blessing. As we embrace these gifts, we recognize them as reflections of God's love, inviting us to live fully in his grace.

This awakening is both humbling and inspiring. Having journeyed through the darkness of addiction, these simple blessings now serve as reminders of how far we've come. Gifts like the ability to fully experience the richness of being human—even in the face of challenges—and the joy of praying to God with grateful hearts are among the most meaningful parts of the spiritual life. Where there was once emptiness, there is now abundance. Each day we choose to embrace the beauty around us, we draw closer to the freedom and restoration God has planned for us.

As we learn to appreciate the small things—those seemingly insignificant moments that are, in fact, profound blessings—we begin to experience the full depth of life in recovery. In this space, we discover that not only is continuing in recovery possible, but it is also a gift to be cherished and celebrated. It's a gift of new eyes to see, a renewed heart to feel, and a revived spirit to embrace all that God has in store for us in our new life.

The path of transformation is a process that is always unfolding. It is where God shapes and refines us with each step we take. As we move forward in recovery, we open ourselves to deeper healing and greater wholeness. Embracing this continual work allows us to become more attuned to the changes God is bringing about in our hearts and lives, guiding us closer to the person he created us to be.

REFLECTION QUESTIONS

1. Recognizing Everyday Blessings: What are some simple gifts from God that you may have overlooked in the past? How can you begin to notice and appreciate these blessings in your life each day?

2. Gratitude as Healing: How does practicing gratitude help shift your focus from pain and loss to peace and healing? In what ways can you actively cultivate a heart of thankfulness in your recovery journey, and how might this transform your daily experience?

3. Embracing the Abundance: How can you more fully embrace the beauty and abundance of life as you walk through your journey? Do you take time to regularly thank God and acknowledge all he has done for you in your life?

FAITH IN ACTION: PRACTICING GRATITUDE

Gratitude is a powerful tool in the recovery journey. It shifts your focus from what you lack or what you struggle with to recognizing what God has already provided. It invites you to celebrate the simple blessings and to see God's hand at work in even the most ordinary moments. Below are some actionable steps to help you practice gratitude in your life, deepening your relationship with God and bringing healing to your heart:

1. Begin Each Day with Thanksgiving
   - Action Step: Start your day by identifying three things you're thankful for—no matter how small. These can be as simple as the warmth of your bed, a cup of coffee, or the sunlight streaming through your window. Writing them down in a journal can help cultivate a mindset of gratitude.

- Why It Matters: Starting your day with thankfulness shifts your focus from what's lacking to what's already present. This practice sets a positive tone for the rest of the day, helping you to see God's blessings even in the ordinary moments.

2. Take Time to Notice the Beauty Around You

   - Action Step: Slow down and engage your senses throughout the day. Pay attention to the beauty of nature—the birds singing, the wind blowing through the trees, the colors of the sky, or the smell of fresh air. Allow these moments to remind you of God's presence and care in your life.

   - Why It Matters: Gratitude thrives in the present moment. By taking time to appreciate the simple beauty around you, you strengthen your awareness of God's goodness and draw closer to him. It also helps you develop a sense of awe and wonder for life itself.

3. Recognize God's Provision in Your Recovery

   - Action Step: Reflect on how far you've come in your recovery journey. Take note of the healing you've experienced, the relationships you've restored, or the new opportunities that have opened up for you. Write these down as reminders of God's faithfulness.

   - Why It Matters: Recognizing God's work in your recovery helps you build confidence in his ongoing provision. Gratitude for past victories strengthens your faith that he will continue to guide you through any challenges that come your way.

4. Create a Daily Gratitude Routine

   - Action Step: Set aside a specific time each day—whether it's in the morning, before meals, or before bed—to say a prayer of thanks. List things you're grateful for and express gratitude for God's love, grace, and the steps you're taking in recovery.

- Why It Matters: Consistent gratitude helps anchor you in a mindset of thankfulness. By making it a regular part of your day, you allow gratitude to shape your perspective and guide your emotional wellbeing, promoting a deep sense of peace and joy.

5. Share Your Gratitude with Others

   - Action Step: Take time to share your thankfulness with the people around you. This could be through a simple "thank you" for something they've done or by expressing gratitude for their presence in your life. Consider sending a note or a message to someone who has been supportive in your recovery.

   - Why It Matters: Gratitude is contagious. By expressing thanks to others, you not only strengthen your relationship with them but also reinforce the practice of gratitude in your own life. It creates a cycle of positive energy and encouragement that uplifts both you and those around you.

6. Reframe Challenges as Opportunities for Growth

   - Action Step: When difficulties arise, choose to view them through the lens of gratitude. Rather than focusing on the hardship, try to see how this challenge might be an opportunity to grow in patience, trust, or resilience. Reflect on how God has used past struggles to refine you.

   - Personal Reflection: I can't emphasize enough how powerful this shift in perspective has been for me. In the past, I would let adversity overwhelm me, getting frustrated or angry. But as I learned to view challenges as opportunities for growth, my spiritual journey took a massive leap forward. Now, even when I'm in the midst of a tough situation, I ask myself what I can learn from it. It may take time—sometimes days or even months—but once I gain clarity, I'm able to take proactive steps to turn that challenge into something beneficial for my personal growth.

This practice has deepened my relationship with God in ways that continue to amaze me.

- Why It Matters: Shifting your perspective on difficulties helps you develop an attitude of gratitude, even in tough times. This doesn't mean ignoring the difficulty but rather finding purpose in the process. It allows you to see that God is using every experience, even the painful ones, to shape you and guide you toward greater growth, trust, and resilience. This mindset enables you to approach future challenges with a sense of peace, knowing that God is always refining you for something greater.

7. Celebrate the Small Moments of Life

- Action Step: Throughout the day, make a conscious effort to celebrate small, seemingly insignificant moments that bring you joy or peace—like enjoying a quiet walk, connecting with a friend, or savoring a meal. Give thanks for these little blessings and allow yourself to fully experience them.

- Why It Matters: Celebrating the small moments helps you stay present and mindful, rather than focusing on what you lack or what's yet to be accomplished. It trains your heart to recognize the fullness of life in the here and now, strengthening your sense of gratitude and contentment.

8. Reflect on God's Faithfulness in Scripture

- Action Step: Spend time in the Bible, specifically focusing on verses that highlight God's faithfulness, provision, and love. Make it a habit to memorize or meditate on verses that inspire gratitude in your heart. Reflect on God's promises and how they've been evident in your own life.

- Why It Matters: Scripture serves as a powerful reminder of God's enduring faithfulness. By meditating on his word, you can deepen your understanding of his character and how he has worked in your past, which strengthens your trust in his continued care and provision for your future.

By actively practicing gratitude, you invite God's peace and presence into every moment. This practice helps you see beauty in the everyday, reminding you that even in the midst of challenges, God is present and working in your life. As you cultivate a heart of gratitude, you will not only deepen your relationship with God but also experience the fullness of life in recovery—appreciating the journey, the process, and the blessings that come each day.

10

The Ongoing Journey of Transformation

AFTER REJECTING WORLDLY INFLUENCES and embracing God's abundant life, it's important to remember that transformation through the LORD is a lifelong process. As we continue to walk in faith, God's grace continually shapes and molds us.

In Philippians, Paul assures us, "And I am sure that he who began a good work in you will bring it to completion at the day of Jesus Christ" (Phil 1:6). The work God has started in us is not finished; it's a daily walk of growth, renewal, and continual surrender. Our growth requires consistent effort, but it is God's strength, not our own, that sustains us.

While the early stages of recovery bring noticeable change, lasting transformation unfolds through our daily choices. We not only thank God but also place our trust in him, lean on the Holy Spirit, and continue to reject the ways of the world. We remind ourselves that true freedom in Christ doesn't mean a life without struggle—it means having the strength to persevere through challenges with God's help. It also means recognizing that we don't face our battles alone but are equipped with the full armor of God. This understanding empowers us to carve our path in the world, guided by the wisdom the Spirit imparts to us.

RENEWAL AND GROWTH: INDIVIDUALLY AND WITHIN THE COMMUNITY

A key driver of continued growth is our ongoing renewal with the Lord. We experience this by reflecting on his word, praying, thanking him daily, and seeking his will over our own desires. As we practice gratitude, it becomes a natural part of our day, strengthening our commitment to living according to God's purpose for our lives.

As we grow, staying connected to the community becomes essential. Recovery is not a solitary journey; we are called to be part of the body of Christ, supporting one another and sharing both challenges and victories in a Christian faith community. We all need our family of God to support us, especially in moments when we are most tempted to return to our former ways. As we heal, we continue to invest in relationships that foster accountability, discipleship, and mutual support. Through fellowship, we encourage one another, share our testimonies, and become instruments of healing in each other's lives.

LIVING OUT OUR TRANSFORMATION: A CALL TO SERVICE

As we continue our journey, we should embrace the responsibility of living out the truths we've discovered in Christ by serving others. As we experience God's grace and transformation, we are called to be agents of change—spreading the hope of the gospel to those still bound by addiction and sharing the freedom we've found in him.

This call to serve others is powerful even though it may seem counterintuitive, especially when we're still in need of healing. But that's the beauty of God's plan—he uses us as instruments to help heal those around us while continuing to heal us. Serving others not only strengthens our relationships but also deepens our own healing as we invest in their journeys.

As we serve others, we discover a more purposeful life, knowing that each day brings us closer to meeting our heavenly Father. Facing life's obstacles or society's challenges becomes easier when we recognize that every day holds the opportunity to fulfill our God-given purpose.

This purpose drives us toward excellence, ensuring that all glory, honor, and praise go to God. While this may be difficult to grasp during active addiction, as we progress in recovery, it becomes more natural. As our life's purpose unfolds and becomes clearer, it eventually becomes our primary motivation, and we come to understand, with every fiber of our being, why God placed us on earth.

New trials will arise as we continue to grow and strive to become more like Christ. Yet, we can face each one with confidence, knowing that God is always with us. No matter where we are on our journey, we can rest assured that he is at work within us and will complete the good work he has begun.

THE POWER OF HOPE AND
TRUST IN GOD'S TIMING

The journey of transformation is rarely smooth. There are times when the road feels long, the steps heavy, and the future uncertain. Yet, it is in these moments that our hope and trust in God's timing become our greatest strength. While the world often promotes instant gratification and quick fixes, recovery and spiritual growth are anything but instant—they are lifelong processes. In this journey, God's timing is always perfect, even when it doesn't align with our expectations.

In our culture, success is often measured by what we achieve and how quickly we achieve it. This mindset can easily spill over into our spiritual lives, leading to frustration when change takes longer than expected. We may wonder why certain struggles persist or why our progress doesn't seem as fast as we'd hoped. However, we must remember that God's timing is always for our ultimate good and his glory. Just as a seed requires time to grow into a tree, our spiritual growth and healing unfold according to his perfect plan. We can trust that God is shaping us into something far greater than we can see at this moment.

Hope is a gift from God that strengthens us to endure through life's toughest seasons. It's not mere optimism based on circumstances but a profound trust in God's faithfulness. As we face life's ups and downs, we can hold fast to the unshakable truth that God is always with us. He has not abandoned us in our struggles, and he never will. Even in our hardest times, God is at work, refining our hearts and deepening our character.

Trusting in God's wisdom and timing requires surrendering our own plans and agendas. It's easy to become impatient, especially when we feel we should be further along, when the future feels uncertain, or when life's biggest questions remain unanswered. Yet, true surrender is about recognizing that God knows what's best for us. We trust that he is not only aware of our circumstances but will use them to create something beautiful within us.

We may never have answers to some of life's most pressing questions—that's simply part of the human experience. Instead of letting this frustrate or anger us, we can choose to accept what we cannot change. In doing so, we open ourselves to a deeper faith in God. Once we realize that much of life is beyond our control, we can shift our focus to the things we can understand, influence, and change. Sobriety offers a unique opportunity to release what no longer serves us. In God's hands, our waiting periods and struggles are never wasted—they are essential to our process of becoming more deeply united with Christ.

SURRENDERING TO GOD'S PERFECT TIMING

As we surrender to God's timing, we are freed from the burden of comparison. In recovery, it's easy to fall into the trap of measuring our progress against others, questioning why their growth seems smoother. But God's work in each of us is unique and our journey is not linear. The story he is writing in our lives is personal, and he is faithful to guide us through each season at the perfect moment.

Embracing God's timing means letting go of the need to compare and trusting that he is at work in our lives, right where we are. Submitting to God's timing brings lasting peace. In a world filled with hurry and pressure, true tranquility is found when we rest in the certainty that God is in control. We don't have to rush our journey or force the process; we can trust that God is guiding us step by step. This peace isn't dependent on our circumstances or how well we think we're doing—it comes from knowing that God is faithful and at work in every moment.

As we trust in God's perfect timing, we can move forward with patience, knowing that he is at work in ways we may not always see or understand. Even when the future is uncertain, we can step out in faith, confident that God holds our future in his hands. We can rest in the truth that he is orchestrating every detail of our recovery and spiritual growth and that his plan will come to completion at the perfect time.

REFLECTION QUESTIONS

1. Commitment to Transformation: How can you stay committed to your journey of transformation, even when faced with setbacks or challenges? Are there areas in your life where you feel tempted to turn back or give up? How can you press forward in faith during those difficult moments?

2. Your Relationship with God: In what ways can you deepen your relationship with God and lean more on his strength for ongoing growth? Are you relying on your own strength in certain areas? If so, how can you fully surrender those challenges to God's power? How can you ensure that you rely on God not only during difficult times but also in times of ease and success?

3. Contributing to the Community: How can you actively contribute to a supportive community that fosters healing and transformation in others? Who in your life could benefit

from the healing and freedom you've found in Christ, and how can you support them on their journey?

4. Perspective Check: When your time on earth comes to an end, you will be *held accountable* before God for all you've done or failed to do in your life. However, there is another perspective: when your time on earth comes to an end, you will have the *opportunity to account* before God for all you've done or chosen not to do. Which perspective will you embrace for the rest of your days?

FAITH IN ACTION: THE ONGOING JOURNEY OF TRANSFORMATION

Spiritual growth and recovery are continuous processes that require intentional, daily steps to keep moving forward. Embracing God's ongoing transformation in your life is a lifelong journey that requires commitment and perseverance. This process will unfold over a lifetime, and to truly grow, you must be willing to embrace it as a long-term commitment. The action steps outlined here are designed to help you live out that transformation in a practical, consistent way. Each step invites you to deepen your connection with God. Through these actions, you actively participate in the renewal he promises, allowing his power to shape and guide you daily.

1. Engage in Consistent Prayer and Reflection

   - Action Step: Set aside a minute or two each day to read an inspirational devotion from a trusted source and pray, reflecting on how God's word applies to your current circumstances. Let this practice shape your mindset and deepen your understanding of his guidance.

   - Personal Reflection: When I was in the depths of my addiction, Friday nights would often send me spiraling. In my years of sobriety, I've intentionally replaced those old patterns with new, Christ-centered activities. Living near an abbey now, I make it a point to visit on Friday evenings for reflective and contemplative prayer and to praise Jesus Christ with the monks. It's become a peaceful way to end my week that helps me stamp out the old, destructive behaviors with new, uplifting ones.

- Why It Matters: Prayer and reflection foster intimacy with God, strengthening your relationship with him. Through this connection, you gain the wisdom and clarity needed to navigate life's challenges. Reflecting on his word not only encourages you but also aligns your decisions with his will, helping you stay grounded and grow in trust.

2. Serve Others with Humility

- Action Step: Find one person or organization where you can serve this week, whether it's through volunteering, helping a neighbor, or simply offering your time and support to someone in need.

- Why It Matters: Serving others is a tangible expression of the love and grace you've received from God. It helps you live out the transformation in your heart by making it visible in your actions. Serving also reminds you that healing isn't just for yourself—it is meant to be shared. It deepens your relationships, fosters community, and makes you more like Christ, who came not to be served but to serve.

3. Connect with a Supportive Faith Community

- Action Step: Attend a Bible study or small group where you can build relationships, share your struggles, and encourage others in their faith.

- Why It Matters: God designed all of us for community, and recovery and spiritual growth thrive in the context of relationships. Being part of a supportive community provides accountability, encouragement, and shared wisdom, which are crucial for your healing and growth.

4. Trust in God's Timing for Healing

- Action Step: Reflect on a current struggle or area of impatience in your life and consciously surrender it to God. Trust that he is at work, even when the process feels slow or uncertain. Remember that God will not abandon you; push through these feelings, knowing they are part of the growing pains that come with an intimate relationship with him.

- Why It Matters: God's timing is perfect, even when it doesn't align with your expectations. Trusting his timing fosters patience and helps you surrender control, which is essential for spiritual growth. By embracing God's wisdom, you can release the desire for instant gratification and find peace in knowing he is shaping you for something greater than you can comprehend in the moment.

5. Cultivate Hope Even in Difficult Times

- Action Step: In moments of struggle, hold fast to the hope that God is using these moments to refine your character. Find joy in knowing that, through him, you are growing stronger.

- Why It Matters: Hope is the anchor that sustains you through difficult seasons. It shifts your perspective from focusing on your circumstances to trusting in God's faithfulness. By cultivating hope, you can endure trials with confidence, knowing that they are part of God's refining process. Hope reminds you that, even when things seem tough, God is working in your life to make you more like Christ.

6. Avoid Comparison and Focus on Your Journey

- Action Step: In moments when you feel tempted to compare, refocus your mind on God's plan for your life. Celebrate your progress and trust that he is working in your specific situation.

- Why It Matters: Comparison steals your joy and leads to dissatisfaction. God's work in each of us is unique, and we are all on a personal journey of transformation. When you focus on your own path and trust God with your journey, you find peace and purpose. Comparison can distract you from God's will and cause unnecessary frustration, but focusing on your own walk helps embrace his perfect plan for your life.

7. Persevere with Confidence

   - Action Step: When faced with difficulty, take a moment to remind yourself of God's faithfulness. Ask him to help you persevere and rely on his strength rather than your own.

   - Why It Matters: Life is filled with challenges, but perseverance is key to spiritual growth. Confidence in God's faithfulness gives you the strength to endure hardships. When you remember that God is always with you and that he has been faithful in the past, you gain the courage to face present and future struggles. Perseverance leads to maturity and helps you grow in character, becoming more like Christ each day.

Embracing God's transformation in your life requires faith, patience, and consistent action. As you commit to these steps, you are not only deepening your relationship with God but also allowing his ongoing work to refine you. It's through each small act of faith that God's work is accomplished in you, drawing you closer to the fullness of his love and purpose.

Final Thoughts

As you reflect on the truths shared in these pages, remember that your journey is a lifelong process—one that requires patience, perseverance, and, above all, a deep reliance on God's grace. There will be ups and downs along the way, but by allowing the Lord to shape you, you'll find the strength to overcome any obstacle. Recovery begins with the courageous first step of surrender, a choice that opens your heart to God's divine love—the only love capable of penetrating deep into your soul and renewing you from the inside out.

God's grace is ever-present, ready to carry you forward into the abundant life he has prepared for you, each and every day. As it says in Lam 3:22–23: "The steadfast love of the Lord never ceases, his mercies never come to an end; they are new every morning; great is your faithfulness." It is through his grace that you find the strength to face each new day, even when the journey feels overwhelming. And through his love, you discover the true essence of your life—one that is no longer bound by slavery to the senses but freed in Christ.

Don't let setbacks or challenges discourage you. Things won't always go as planned, and at times, it may feel like nothing is working. But remember to pause and seek the good in every situation, no matter how difficult it may seem. Your attitude has the power to make all the difference.

If you find yourself frustrated with the pace of your recovery, remember that each moment holds valuable lessons—lessons that often require careful reflection before you can confidently move to the next stage of your journey. This process of discernment involves paying attention to the subtle ways God is shaping you, recognizing the lessons hidden within your struggles and learning to hear his guidance amid uncertainty. As you take time to understand what God is teaching you, the wisdom gained from past experiences will build upon itself, preparing you for what lies ahead. Your walk with God is like learning any new skill: the more you practice, the better you become. Mistakes are not weaknesses; when approached with a positive attitude, they become opportunities for growth. Just as we don't expect a child to walk before crawling, it's important to keep things in perspective.

Remember to trust in God's perfect timing, especially when impatience begins to creep in. Set aside time throughout your busy day to seek his guidance. Surrender, without reservation, the parts of your heart you've kept hidden—the ones that still feel broken or unworthy. Let his light shine into the darkest corners of your soul, bringing the healing and peace you deserve. With each step you take, no matter how small, trust that you are never alone.

Recovery is a journey of restoration where you embrace your true identity in Christ—beloved, immeasurably valued, and called to a purpose far greater than you could ever imagine. As you walk this path, remember that the LORD is with you every step of the way, guiding, strengthening, and renewing you. Through him, you are being transformed into the person God has always meant for you to be, reflecting his love and grace to the world around you.

No matter where you are in your recovery, remember that God's work in your life is far from finished. The road ahead holds more growth and freedom than you may have ever believed possible. As you gain momentum in your new life, you'll look back and hardly recognize the old you—because with him, through him, and in him, you are stepping into the abundant, prosperous life God has set before you in Christ. In time, you will realize that everything you've been through has shaped you into the warrior you are becoming.

Your journey is uniquely yours, marked by both struggles and triumphs—each one molding you into the incredible person God created you to be. Every step, no matter how challenging, carries purpose and beauty. With Christ leading the way, you are destined for greatness!

If you take away just one thing from this book, let it be this: in a world that often feels broken and upside-down, the answers to your questions are already within you. When you turn to the Holy Spirit as your Counselor, he will guide you every step of the way—always.

God bless you.

Index

Scripture by Theme

OLD TESTAMENT

NEW TESTAMENT

INDEX